YOUR HEART IS IN YOUR HANDS

DR. MILLIE LEE, MD, FACC

WHAT PEOPLE ARE SAYING:

"This kind of integrative approach is the future of medicine, but with her guidance, you can have it today."
Timothy McCall, MD
Author of *Yoga as Medicine: The Yogic Prescription for Health and Healing* and *Saving My Neck: A Doctor's East/West Journey through Cancer*
Medical Editor, *Yoga Journal*

"Do you want to gain control of your health and well-being? Look no further than this powerful book!"
Wendy K. Benson, MBA, OTR/L and Elizabeth A. Myers, RN
Co-Authors, The Confident Patient
2x2 Health: Private Health Concierge

"The most readable, most current and most comprehensive summary of what contributes to heart disease."
- Liz Lyster, MD
- Doctor, Best-Selling Author, Speaker

"If you believe you hold the power to take an active part in preventing or reversing disease in your body, then this book is for you!"
Linda F. Patten, Leadership Trainer for Women Entrepreneurs and Changemakers – President & CEO

"Dr. Lee expertly navigates the multi-faceted nature of the heart as a physical and energetic entity."
Pooja Amy Shah, MD
Integrative Medicine

"This book explains the five root causes of heart disease called the Heart Matrix that are connected and influence heart health."
Patricia J. Rullo
Patient Safety Author/Speaker/Radio Host

"This book is a timely gift, an eye and heart opener."
Lorraine Giordano
Founder, Inspired To Health

"Her inspiring, innovative, patient-centered approach to heart disease is a game-changer for reversing and preventing heart disease."
Marlene Elizabeth
Author, Certified Money Coach®

"Dr. Lee masters the art of teaching scientific information in the simplest ways."
Carol Fitzgerald
Author, Health Care Advocate

Your Heart Is In Your Hands

Copyright © 2020 by Dr. Millie Lee, MD, FACC

RHG Media Productions
25495 Southwick Drive #103
Hayward, CA 94544.

ISBN 978-0-578-69854-0 (paperback)

Visit us on line at www.YourPurposeDrivenPractice.com

Printed in the United States of America.

ENDORSEMENT

D r. Millie Lee's book, *Your Heart Is in Your Hands*, draws from her own experiences and lessons as a cardiologist and functional medicine doctor. Dr. Lee's book provides important information for those of us who want to prevent and reverse heart disease. With half of all Americans at risk for heart disease, I believe this book is a must-read and highly recommend it.

Mark Hyman, MD
#1 New York Times Bestselling Author of *Food: What the Heck Should I Eat?*
Head of Strategy and Innovation, Cleveland Clinic Center for Functional Medicine

TABLE OF CONTENTS

DISCLAIMER

This book is not intended as a substitute for the medical advice of physicians. The ideas, procedures, and suggestions contained in this book are not intended as a substitute treatment for physical, emotional or medical problems without the advice of a physician, either directly or indirectly. The intent of the author is only to offer information of a general nature to help you in your quest for physical and emotional well-being. The reader should regularly consult a physician in matters relating to his/her health and particularly with respect to any symptoms that may require diagnosis or medical attention. In the event you use any of the information in this book for yourself, the author and the publisher assume no responsibility for your actions.

ACKNOWLEDGEMENTS

I thank and honor all those who helped me bring this book to life. Rebecca Hall Gruyter, my publisher, thank you for guiding me along every step of the publishing process and empowering me to share my vision. Thank you to the RHG publishing team for your wonderful work and patience with my multiple book cover revisions. I am so grateful to my creative and brilliant friend Jess Cherry who helped me spread the powerful message on unfamiliar platforms.

I would not be who I am without the love and support of my family, especially my parents, my biggest cheerleaders who taught me that all things are possible. Mom, thank you for always being the wind beneath my wings. Dad, thank you for your eternal optimism. Jenny, thank you for being my sunshine, the yin to my yang, the frick to my frack. Although you are my baby sister, your faith and wisdom have helped guide me along this incredible journey.

To my professional mentors at Columbia-Presbyterian Medical Center, Dr. Elsa-Grace Giardina, Dr. Mark Apfelbaum, and Dr. Hal Wasserman, thank you for your faith in me. To my patients, thank you for entrusting your hearts in my hands and for the privilege of being your physician.

To my yoga and spiritual guides thank you for enlightening me. One of the biggest turning points in my life was recognizing that my dharma was to integrate and share everything I have learned from the medical world and the yoga world. A special thanks to John and Chris Yax and their beautiful family for changing my life. Thank you, Dr. Timothy McCall, author of *Yoga as Medicine*, and Dr. Dilip Sarkar for leading the way. Thank you, Mala Cunningham, for your endless encouragement. To my teachers Dana Slamp and

Sonja Rzepski, thank you for guiding me further along my dharmic journey and making the integration of cardiology and yoga possible.

FOREWORD

My grandmother went blind in her 40s as a result of diabetes. That, and the fact that my family background is rife with heart disease, cancer & diabetes, was the impetus for me to change my way of eating many years ago.

"Are you saying you can take charge of your health and wellbeing and avert disease merely by changing your way of eating?" Yes, indeed, that's exactly what I am saying and what Dr. Millie Lee says in her very powerful book, *Your Heart Is in Your Hands*.

As a healthcare advocate, I follow many of the doctors who teach that heart disease and other diseases are not only preventable, but also reversible.

I reasoned that if I eat what my family ate, I will get what they got. If not, I have a better chance. I read a book called *Brain Trust: The Hidden Connection Between Mad Cow and Misdiagnosed Alzheimer's Disease* by Colm Kelleher that put me on this path. When I finished the book, I said to myself, "I am never eating another piece of beef or pork again." I continued to study and research the rest of that year, *never, ever* having any intention whatsoever to change anything else in my diet.

I'm Italian and have always enjoyed the good old "standard American diet." I ate everything from beef to chicken to pork to fish and everything in between. In fact, I'd written a cookbook with all the wonderful "standard American diet" recipes. Everyone *loved* my cooking and my food.

However, I didn't feel justified publishing it because one fine morning, I woke up and said, "Everything else is going, too." It's been 16 years. And I feel wonderful. No aches or pains, generally speaking, unless I hurt myself dancing or doing yoga.

Further, I am on no medications, which is a rarity in itself. If and when I do get a cold, few and far between, they are never full-blown and do not last very long. An injury is always treated with myofascial release treatments or energy treatments or some natural modality.

I rarely visit a doctor. My body is sound and healthy. My mother passed away at the age of 102. Though there are no guarantees, I have longevity. If I do live to a ripe old age such as that, I want it to be healthy. Thus, what I do is mainly for prevention.

I have since written another cookbook: *You Don't Have to be Vegan to Enjoy These Meals*. Though I've read many books like this, Dr. Lee's *Your Heart Is in Your Hands* was totally in alignment with what I believe. I smiled to myself when I saw what it was about.

While books like this tend to put some people to sleep, I find them juicy, and I couldn't wait to get into it. LOL!

If you, dear reader, are looking for a way out of ill health or merely want to prevent it, do yourself a favor and read this book to get and keep you on a path to good and excellent health. I say in my book, "Getting old does not have to mean getting sick. Sickness is not an inevitable fact of life. Our bodies are wonderful machines and given the right foods can actually propel us on the path to good health."

Take care, Dr. Lee, and keep changing people's lives. I congratulate and admire you for stepping out of the mainstream to tell the truth. Thank you for saying yes when you got the nudge to write this book so that others can know that good health is possible.

Carol Fitzgerald
Author
Health Care Advocate
www.carolfitzgerald.net
Youtube: www.youtube.com/user/thecarobi5
Facebook: www.facebook.com/carol.fitzgerald.357
Instagram: @carolfitzgerald5

INTRODUCTION
THE HEART OF THE MATTER

"The heart of man is very much like the sea, it has its storms, it has its tides, and in its depths it has its pearls, too."
~Vincent van Gogh

I have often been asked why I became a cardiologist. As a child, I had no doctor role models growing up. It was in medical school that I fell in love with the heart. Everything about the heart fascinated me—its anatomy, function and resilience. I remember observing open heart surgery and watching the cardiothoracic surgeons work on a beating heart. It blew my mind. The first two years of medical school are spent in the classroom and laboratories with very little exposure to patients. This is when I fell in love with the science of everything heart related. The third and fourth years of medical school are your "clinical" years where you work with live patients. During my cardiology rotation, I saw everything from heart attacks to congenital heart defects. What struck me the most was how quickly patients could recover from most cardiac conditions as compared to other medical conditions. It was then that I knew I wanted to be a cardiologist. I loved the idea of "fixing" patients so they could quickly resume their lives.

The heart is an extraordinary part of our bodies that we cannot live without. Its function is quite simply to keep us alive. Life begins with the first heartbeat and ends with the last. The heart is a muscular organ that pumps blood, rich in nutrients and oxygen, to every other cell in our bodies. It is the hardest working muscle in the body, working twenty-four hours a day, seven days a week, without pausing. And unlike other organs, the heart has little regenerative capacity. So when the heart is damaged, for example after a heart attack, the result can be permanent.

The heart is also, metaphorically speaking, the center of intuition, wisdom and connection. We often refer to this heart when we say "listen to your heart" or "speak from your heart." This is your emotional heart providing you with valuable information and guidance. Fascinating research by Dr. Rollin McCraty at the Institute of HeartMath has shown that the heart rhythm of the physical heart reflects a person's emotional state.[1] And the heart's large electromagnetic field, which is influenced by our emotions, sends signals to not only our own brains, but to those around us, accounting for that feeling that you get around certain people in different emotional states. **If people knew more about the critical role the heart plays in our lives, I believe they would do whatever it takes to protect this precious gem living within all of us.**

Heart disease remains the leading cause of death globally.[2] About 640,000 Americans die from heart disease each year—that is 1 out of every 4 deaths, affecting all genders and ethnicities.[3] Nearly half of all Americans have some form of Cardiovascular Disease, and half of all Americans have at least one risk factor for heart disease and may not even be aware of it.[4]

The 20th century is noted for its many technological advances and nowhere has it been more impactful than in medicine. Death from cardiovascular disease declined

---

1. McCraty R et al. The effects of emotions on short-term power spectrum analysis of heart rate variability. American Journal Card 1995; 76(14):1089-1093

2. Heron M. Deaths: Leading causes for 2017.national Vital Statistics Reports; 68(6)

3. Benjamin EJ et al. Heart disease and stroke statistics - 2019. A report from the American Heart Association. Circulation 2019; 139(10): e56-528

4. Fryar CD et al. Prevalence of uncontrolled risk factors for cardiovascular disease. United States. 1999-2010. NCHS data brief, no 103

significantly from 1950 to 2005, in part due to the infusion of advanced technology into cardiac care. But it is also due to an improvement in health which was driven predominantly by a significant decline in cigarette smoking. Mortality from heart disease plateaued in the beginning of this century, and now the prevalence of heart disease and death are on the rise again. And the rise is not in the baby boomer generation as one might suspect, but in adults ages 35-64: our workforce, our parents and our caregivers.

So this is a real problem that we should not ignore. Every 40 seconds, someone in the United States is having a heart attack.[3] Every minute, more than one person dies of a cardiac event.[3] In addition to the toll heart disease exacts on our health, the economic burden is enormous. In 2016, the cost of Cardiovascular Disease was $555 billion. It is projected that by 2035, the cost will skyrocket to $1.1 trillion.[5]

Most of this money is spent on medications, procedures, physicians and hospitalizations for the acute and advanced stages of heart disease. Imagine if we could detect heart disease at the early stages or prevent it all together. What effect would that have on our lives, our society, our country and our planet? Well, I believe we can. This book provides the information to support you in determining your own risk for heart disease. It is also intended to empower the reader to protect their hearts through simple lifestyle choices.

5. Benjamin EJ et al. Heart disease and stroke statistics - 2019 update: a report from the American Heart Association. Circulation 2019; 139(10): e56-528

PART I. HEART DISEASE

THE TRADITIONAL VIEW OF HEART DISEASE

After I completed medical school, I spent eight years at Columbia-Presbyterian Medical Center in NY learning everything I could about heart disease. I had incredible teachers, mentors, patients and colleagues that propelled me forward to being chief cardiology fellow and the first female interventional fellow at Columbia-Presbyterian, an honor I did not take lightly. My job was, for the most part, to perform cardiac catheterizations, including coronary angiograms to determine the severity of coronary artery disease (CAD), and in patients with unstable disease or heart attacks, open the blocked arteries. At that time, I believed with all my heart that this career path would allow me to "fix" heart disease.

The most common type of heart disease is Coronary Artery Disease (or CAD), and this is the subject that I will mostly focus on in this book. Coronary artery disease is often responsible for the other forms of heart disease such as heart failure and arrhythmias. As the name implies, Coronary Artery Disease is disease of the coronary arteries—the arteries that supply blood to the heart itself. The term Cardiovascular disease is often used interchangeably but also includes strokes (involving the arteries of the brain) and hypertension (high blood pressure). CAD develops as a result of Atherosclerosis, a word derived from two Greek roots: 'athere' meaning gruel and 'sclerosis' meaning hardening. So atherosclerosis is literally 'hardening of the arteries', which is due to accumulation of cholesterol and other substances in the wall of the arteries. The focal accumulation of these substances is referred to as "plaque".

As an interventional cardiologist, I witnessed first-hand the detrimental effects heart disease has on the many lives it touches. After my training, I moved to Virginia where I practiced interventional cardiology for 18 years. In the past 20 years, I have treated thousands of patients with heart disease. Most of my time was spent in the hospital taking care of acute problems—heart attacks, heart failure, arrhythmias. In fact, I met most of my patients in the hospital. I was on call for anyone who came to the emergency room having a heart attack. A heart attack generally happens when one of the heart arteries suddenly is occluded with a blood clot. When the artery is occluded, the heart muscle can die very quickly, which is why we had little time to act knowing that "time is muscle." The goal is to get the artery open in less than 90 minutes, preferably 60 minutes from the time of presentation. This was generally done by rushing the patients to the cardiac catheterization laboratory, putting a catheter in an artery of the leg or arm that would allow further catheters to be advanced right to the arteries of the heart where contrast (dye) was injected and the blockage or blockages identified. While some patients require emergent bypass surgery, most patients having a heart attack are treated with a procedure called percutaneous coronary intervention or PCI. A balloon is inflated at the site of blockage, opening the artery and restoring blood flow. Nine out of ten times, a stent (a small metal coil) is implanted at the site to keep the artery open. As you can imagine, this life saving process does not allow much time to talk and get to know your patient.

The majority of patients felt immediately better after their percutaneous coronary intervention and would go home in a couple of days and resume their lives. A satisfying result for all involved. But then I would see these same patients in my office a couple of weeks later and come to find that they haven't altered their lifestyles in any significant way and their risk factors remained the same, putting them at very high risk for recurrent events and death. **While initially frustrated, I realized that it was not their fault, that we, the healthcare**

system had failed them, and due to the constraints of our healthcare system, the focus wasn't as strongly aimed at their lifestyles. When they were discharged from the hospital, they were given a list of dos and don'ts and at least four new medications. Cardiac rehab was recommended to all patients but many of my patients could not afford to take time off from work to attend the classes, and perhaps we failed to emphasize the importance of cardiac rehab or offer good alternatives.

One of the major weaknesses of our current healthcare system is lack of time. One of the biggest complaints patients have when visiting medical offices is not having enough time with the provider and not being heard. Sadly, medical providers are incentivized, not for quality but quantity, meaning the number of patient encounters. In my old office, hospital follow-up visits were allotted 15 minutes. Most of this time was used by the nurse to obtain vital signs and reconcile medications in the electronic medical records. There was very little time left for the patient-doctor interaction. It's no wonder that their lifestyles hadn't changed very much. Every single patient was "stressed out" after these frightening cardiac events. Yet, there was not enough time to address it in a meaningful way.

I came to realize that heart disease is not an acute disease, easily fixed with a stent and "optimal medical therapy," but rather a chronic disease and a lifestyle disease. It only presents acutely, often when it is too late. Don't get me wrong, these procedures and medications can be life-saving when patients are having a heart attack and often necessary when patients have severe symptoms not manageable by standard medical care. But **heart disease is a chronic disease, and I believe this demands a new approach to its prevention and management.**

The conventional approach to patients with heart disease is symptom relief and secondary prevention (after an event) of recurrent events and associated complications such as heart failure, arrhythmias and death. Little to no effort is applied to its reversal and prevention.

I believe heart disease can be reversed and prevented. Believe it or not, the bold statement that heart disease is reversible is not a new concept. In a landmark trial, the Lifestyle Heart Trial, Dr. Dean Ornish demonstrated in a group of patients with moderate CAD, a statistically significant regression of blockages, not with drugs, but with intensive lifestyle changes.[6] Dr. Ornish has been and continues to be a pioneer in this field. In fact, he started offering his lifestyle program to cardiac patients in the 1970s and published the Lifestyle Heart Trial in 1990. Unfortunately, this did not translate immediately into behavioral changes for patients, doctors or hospitals. Only after demonstrating sustained benefit (5 years) and **cost savings** in patients following his program (and significant worsening of the group following standard protocol) did Centers for Medicare & Medicaid Services (CMS) decide to include the Ornish program as a covered intensive cardiac rehab program.

For many, the development of heart disease seems almost inevitable, whether that be due to a family history of heart disease or the presence of a risk factor associated with a higher risk of heart disease. But coronary artery disease is preventable! Eighty percent of CAD is believed to be preventable with standard care recommendations. I would say it is nearly all preventable with intensive lifestyle modifications.

---

6. Ornish D. The Lifestyle Heart Trial. Lancet 1990; 336: 129-133.

THE HEART MATRIX

"In nature everything is connected, interwo-
ven, subject to natural law. We cannot separate our-
selves from that, no matter how hard we try."
~Jeffrey R. Anderson

Along life's journey, I was introduced to yoga. Like many Americans, I started to practice yoga for the physical benefits but quickly noticed the effect it had on my mind and spirit. Life as a doctor can feel very stressful, and yoga helped me manage my stress. I was hooked and I wanted to learn more, so I did my first teacher training, which taught me so much more than physical poses and flexibility.

I learned that yoga is a way of life, a lifestyle that reflects all aspects of our lives, including how we relate to others, take care of ourselves, eat, breath, move and find peace in our stressful lives. **I began to live this lifestyle and thought that my patients could benefit from this type of lifestyle as well.** I can honestly say that this was a turning point in my life. In yoga, there is a concept known as Dharma—your purpose in life. For years I had the sense that being an interventional cardiologist was not my ultimate dharma. Then the prover- bial light bulb shone brightly. **My dharma is to marry my two worlds—to integrate the science of Western medicine with the ancient wisdom of yoga.** As a cardiologist, I was espe- cially awed at the magnitude of research that supported the benefits of yoga for heart disease and many chronic diseases. **I realized everything I had learned and done in my career as a cardiologist was part of my journey to my dharma.**

I studied more yoga, especially therapeutic yoga and cardiac yoga, meditation, Ayurveda, nutrition and Functional Medicine which helped me put it all together. **All of these wonderful**

healing practices have taught me one important lesson—seeing each person in front of me as a unique soul with a unique history, way of life and health needs. This is in stark contrast to the reductionistic model of conventional medicine.

In conventional medicine, management of disease is "reduced" down to the smallest part. Meaning the care becomes focused on the part of the body showing symptoms, not the body as a whole. When I had a painful, torn meniscus in my knee I saw an orthopedic surgeon who operated on my knee. A few years later, I developed a rotator cuff tear and thought I could see the same specialist, but I was told that he only deals with knees and that I would have to see someone who deals with shoulders. Interestingly, these limbs are even further reduced—the leg is reduced to the foot, the knee and the hip, each with its own specialist. **Our bodies however are so much more than the sum of its parts. We are complex beings with multiple organ systems, feelings, emotions and thoughts that function together to create a "whole" person.**

In Functional Medicine, we dig deep to uncover the root causes of disease and integrate all systems. It is not enough to treat each person with a heart attack with the standard protocol of stents and drugs. As doctors we have to ask why. Why, for example, does a young person without any traditional risk factors suffer a heart attack? For decades, cholesterol has been demonized as the principle cause of heart disease, and if your blood cholesterol levels were normal, either naturally or with medication, and your doctor told you everything looked good, then you assumed that you were safe from heart disease. But this is far from the truth. Functional Medicine looks at the "whole" individual, understanding the interconnection of all our body systems regardless of where a condition or disease manifests and I take this approach with my patients. I factor in what is going on in an individual's life in body, mind and spirit.

I like to look at heart disease as a dynamic interplay of five root elements—five conditions that are not traditionally

addressed in conventional cardiology that collectively I call the Heart Matrix. The five elements correspond to dysfunction in five major body systems that are intricately connected to the heart—immune system, nervous system, digestive system, endocrine (hormone) system and genetics. **Our bodies are like the five elements of nature—Earth, Water, Fire, Air and Space.** They function together to create how we experience nature, and that nature changes every day. Consider how these elements interact with each other to create our weather patterns. Our weather patterns are dictated by the interplay of moisture (water), temperature (fire), wind (air) and the position of Earth in the solar system (earth and space). Storms occur when these elements are out of balance.

Our bodies, consisting of the same elements, behave in much the same way. **An imbalance in one or more of the systems can result in stormy health or disease.** The Heart Matrix is made up of five elements or conditions (system imbalances) that can independently cause heart disease but that are also intrinsically connected with each other and can turn each other on, creating a synergistic effect on the heart. These five conditions that I will discuss in much greater detail throughout the book are Inflammation (Fire), Digestive Disorders, such as Leaky Gut and Dysbiosis (Earth), Insulin Resistance (Water), Stress (Air) and Genetics/Epigenetics (Space).

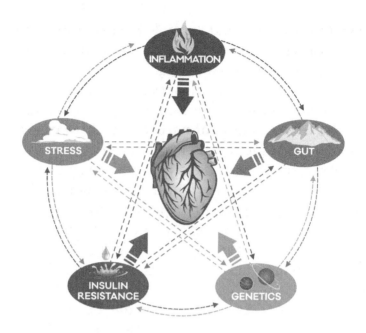

As you can see, these are not the usual suspects, such as high cholesterol and high blood pressure. The usual suspects are very important to know, but they, too, have the same root causes and can be largely prevented. The usual suspects are akin to the check engine light in your car. They are warning signs that require further investigation. They are not the root causes of heart disease. The traditional approach to these risk factors is to treat them medically and the buck stops there. I believe a deeper and more whole-body system approach is needed.

Heart disease (like all chronic diseases) is the result of a complex network of systems that have gone haywire. Heart disease is not a linear equation of

High Cholesterol = Heart Disease

Or

Low Cholesterol = Heart Health

Using the Heart Matrix, we can see that the five elements, the five root causes are connected and influence each other.

For example, inflammation and stress are root causes of heart disease. Not only do they independently cause heart disease, but stress causes inflammation and inflammation causes stress. Now you have two root causes of disease amplifying your risk. See how this works?

IT'S NOT ALL ABOUT THE PLUMBING

Cardiologists often describe the heart as a house, met- aphorically speaking. The coronary arteries of the heart are considered the plumbing. The rhythm of the heartbeat is considered the electrical system and the heart muscle is the water pump. Pretty reductionistic, I know. And unfortunately, the management of coronary artery disease has been reduced to treating the coronary arteries as pipes. My colleagues and I were often referred to as the plumbers. We even used a tool called a "roto-rooter" to cut out heavily calcified plaque in the arteries. Other colleagues who spe- cialize in heart rhythm abnormalities are referred to as the electricians. But the truth is that CAD is more complex than simple plumbing and the root cause of disease may not even be in the "pipes".

Atherosclerosis, the clogging or hardening of arteries, has for centuries been thought to be the "cause" of coronary heart disease. The arteries are clogged by <u>plaques</u>—a "gru- el"-like accumulation of fatty deposits and cholesterol within the wall of the arteries. It also contains other cells and sub- stances, such as smooth muscle cells, collagen, white blood cells, immune cells and calcium. Atherosclerosis is the mani- festation, not the cause, of heart disease. I query "What is the root cause of the atherosclerosis?" This query led me to write this book.

The Traditional View

The clogging of the arteries is often described as a block- age obstructing blood flow to the heart (or in the case of a stroke, the brain). These blockages are usually quantified as a percentage of narrowing of the central lumen through which blood flows (stenosis). For example, a 100 percent stenosis is complete blockage of the central lumen (no flow of blood), which results in a heart attack and permanent heart damage if not treated within hours. A 50 percent stenosis is narrowing of the central lumen by half. You can think of these plaques that bulge into the center of the arteries as small volcanoes protruding from the earth.

Underneath the fibrous cap (or crater) lies the magma—a combination of fats and cholesterol, smooth muscle cells, collagen, calcium AND inflammatory cells. A heart attack occurs much like a volcano erosion. When the heat and pressure rise, which in the case of CAD is inflammation, the plaque ruptures. Blood cells such as platelets rush in to control the bleeding, clump together and the resulting blood clot is what occludes the artery, resulting in a heart attack or myocardial infarction.

The truth is that atherosclerosis begins way before we see any obstruction of blood flow and even before we see plaque. Changes in function likely precede changes in structure. All arteries are made up of three layers. The innermost layer that is in contact with the flowing blood is called the intima. It is in this layer that atherosclerotic plaques are found. The intima consists of a thin (one cell thick) inner lining called the endothelium and a sub endothelial layer. The endothelium lines the inside of every blood vessel in the body and the inside of the heart chambers, making it quite extensive. If all the endothelium in an adult body were to be spread out, it would take up the area of eight tennis courts.

The endothelium is a protective, highly active and dynamic tissue producing many factors (most notably nitric oxide) that regulate vascular tone, barrier function and inhibit platelet clumping or aggregation, oxidative stress and inflammation. The main function is to provide a selectively permeable barrier between the blood and the rest of the vessel, only allowing entry of essential cells and nutrients. LDL cholesterol can only exert its harm if it manages to penetrate the endothelial barrier. There is growing evidence that atherosclerosis begins in the **endothelium**. Injury to the endothelium and endothelial dysfunction are the earliest signs of atherosclerosis.

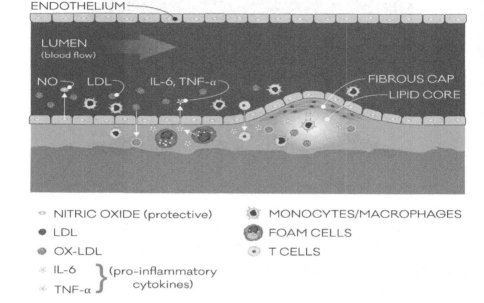

NITRIC OXIDE (protective)
LDL
OX-LDL
IL-6 } (pro-inflammatory
TNF-α } cytokines)

MONOCYTES/MACROPHAGES
FOAM CELLS
T CELLS

Atherosclerotic plaque progression. Normal endothelial cells produce nitric oxide, which is cardioprotective. Endothelial dysfunction permits LDL cholesterol and immune cells (monocytes) to enter the arterial wall. Within the intima, the immune cells which eat up the cholesterol produce pro-inflammatory chemicals called cytokines.

An important point to make here is that these plaques need not be obstructive to cause a heart attack! In fact, the plaques that rupture and cause the most damage, i.e., heart attack, are lesions less than 50 percent in stenosis. Research continues to expand our knowledge of what is really going on inside these plaques and inside the arteries as a whole. Importantly, we know that atherosclerosis is a progressive condition that begins with changes in the arterial wall (both structure and function), without any obstruction at all and without any symptoms or clinical manifestations.

It is becoming more widely accepted that atherosclerosis is more of an inflammatory process than an excess of cholesterol. Markers of inflammation have been identified at every stage of atherosclerosis, from the beginning stages (even identified in children), silently under the surface, within the walls of the arteries, to severe blockages and heart attack. Traditional diagnostic tests, like stress tests and cardiac catheterizations are looking for indirect (stress test) or direct evidence (catheterization) of a significant (greater than 70 percent) blockage. While these percentages sound high, these blockages are generally the more stable lesions and less likely to rupture. And yet these are the blockages that are treated with stents and bypass surgery. The lesions that cause heart attacks are usually no more than 50 percent obstructive, and these cannot be detected by stress tests. So how do we determine who is really at risk for a heart attack?

RISK FACTORS VS ROOT CAUSES

"Life is like a tree . . . once we tend the root,
the tree as a whole will be healthy."
~Deepak Chopra

The traditional way of evaluating someone for heart disease is to determine if they have risk factors and calculate their risk for a major event based solely on those risk factors. The traditional five risk factors include cigarette smoking, high cholesterol, high blood pressure, diabetes and age. These factors are plugged into an algorithm called the Framingham Risk Assessment Tool or similar scoring tool. This tool uses information from the Framingham Heart Study to predict your risk of developing a heart attack or death from coronary artery disease in the next ten years.

Glaringly missing from this assessment tool are obesity, physical inactivity, and family history of heart disease, well established risk factors. Also missing are less well-established risk factors or the root causes, what I call the five root elements of the Heart Matrix—Inflammation, Stress, Insulin Resistance, Gut Abnormalities and Genetics.

The Functional Medicine approach seeks to identify the root cause of heart disease, which means getting to the root cause of all the risk factors. So what does this look like?

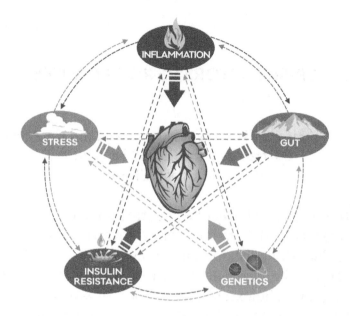

    In this model, the root cause of almost all the risk factors and thus heart disease is an interplay of Stress, Inflammation, Gut Abnormalities, Insulin Resistance and Genetics. For some people, one or more of these factors may predominate, but as the diagram illustrates, they influence each other.

    For example, chronic stress leads to elevated levels of the hormone cortisol in our body. Cortisol, in turn, leads to elevated blood glucose levels which may lead to insulin resistance. Insulin is the hormone that helps get glucose into our cells for energy. When insulin resistance exists (which is also due to inflammation), the cells do not recognize insulin, and the blood glucose can't enter the cells (excess glucose is converted to fat), which may ultimately result in obesity, metabolic syndrome and diabetes. Cortisol also activates the immune system, which when done in the setting of chronic stress leads to inflammation, as in the gut and in adipose (fat) tissue. An inflamed, leaky gut and inflamed adipose tissue then allow further inflammatory substances to enter the bloodstream where they play a role in the activation and progression of atherosclerosis. **The good news is that I believe by getting to the root cause or causes we are able to reverse these risk factors and improve your health.**

PART II. ARE YOU AT RISK FOR HEART DISEASE?

"An awareness of one's mortality can lead you to wake up and live an authentic, meaningful life."
~Bernie Siegel

About half of all Americans have at least one of the traditional risk factors for heart disease.[7] I suspect even more people have the risk factors that I will discuss in this book. Most of these risk factors have something to do with how we live our lives and demonstrate how our lifestyles influence our mind, body and spirit. **The more risk factors you have, the greater your risk for developing heart disease. The good news is that they are ALL modifiable, even your genetics.** I will begin with the traditional risk factors because they are important to be aware of and modify. Then I will discuss the five root elements of the heart matrix.

---

7. Fryar CD et al. Prevalence of uncontrolled risk factors for cardiovascular disease: United States. 1999-2010

CIGARETTE SMOKING

I think it is safe to say that everyone knows that smoking is not good for your health. But perhaps you may not know how it increases your risk for heart disease. The chemicals in tobacco smoke directly harm your blood cells. They can also damage the structure and the function of your blood vessels, increasing your risk for atherosclerosis. Any amount of smoking, even light smoking or "social" smoking can cause damage to the heart and blood vessels. Secondhand smoke also raises your risk of heart disease, as you are still breathing it in.

The persistent campaign over the past several decades against the harmful and deadly effects of tobacco resulted in not only a reduction in cigarette smoking but reduced rates of death from cardiovascular and lung disease. Smoking rates have dropped by 67 percent since 1965, when the National Health Interview Survey (NHIS) first began tracking it. While it is true that cigarette smoking rates in the United States are the lowest they've ever been, one in five Americans (about 34 million) still use some tobacco products.[8]

These statistics do not even include those Americans who have taken up the unhealthy habit of vaping. While e-cigarettes do not contain tobacco, they still contain nicotine, which is addictive and toxic. They also include other chemicals that are toxic to the heart and lungs.

Despite the progress, cigarette smoking remains the leading preventable cause of disease and death in the United States. Cigarette smoking has been linked to numerous

---

8. Creamer MR et al. Tobacco Product Use and Cessation Indicators Among Adults - United States. 2018. Morbidity and Mortality Weekly Report 2019, 68(45); 1013-1019

illnesses, including heart disease, high blood pressure, stroke, chronic obstructive pulmonary disease and cancer. I believe continued population-based interventions are needed to lower smoking rates even further.

One of the best ways to reduce your risk of heart disease if you currently smoke is to quit. I appreciate that both tobacco and nicotine are addictive, but quitting is possible, and no matter how much or how long you've smoked, quitting will lower your risk of developing and dying from heart disease. There are several strategies and programs available that can help you quit. I definitely recommend getting support from friends, family, healthcare professionals or support groups (offered by many local hospitals, American Heart Association, and the American Cancer Society). If you don't smoke, do your best to avoid secondhand smoke.

HYPERTENSION

Hypertension, or high blood pressure, is a major mod-ifiable risk factor for heart disease and premature death. At least 30 percent of Americans have high blood pressure.[9] Blood pressure (BP) is the pressure or force within your arteries. When you have your blood pressure checked, you will see two numbers reported. The top number is your systolic pressure, the pressure in the arteries when the heart is contracting. The bottom number is the diastolic pressure, the pressure in the arteries when the heart is resting between contractions. Normal blood pressure is 120/80 mm Hg. High blood pressure is defined as a systolic BP $\geq$ 130 mm Hg or diastolic BP > 80 mm Hg.

In about one in twenty cases of hypertension, high blood pressure occurs as the result of an underlying condition, medication or drug.[10] Conditions[11] that can cause high blood pressure include kidney disease, diabetes, obstructive sleep apnea, and certain hormonal disorders such as thyroid or adrenal disease. Medications and drugs that can increase your blood pressure include non-steroidal anti-inflammatory drugs (NSAIDs) such as ibuprofen and naproxen, steroids,

9. Fryar CD et al. Hypertension Prevalence and Control Among Adults: United States, 2015-2016. National Center for Health Statistics Data Brief No. 289, October 2017

10. Chobanian AV et al. Joint National Committee on Prevention, Detection, Evaluation, and Treatment of High Blood Pressure: National Heart, Lung, and Blood Institute; National High Blood Pressure Education Program Coordinating Committee. Seventh report of the Joint National Committee on Prevention, Detection, Evaluation, and Treatment of High Blood Pressure. Hypertension. 2003; 42(6): 1206-1252

11. Omura M et al. Prospective study on the prevalence of secondary hypertension among hypertensive patients visiting a general outpatient clinic in Japan. Hypertension Res. 2004;27(3): 193-202

oral contraceptives, some antidepressants, some over the counter cough and cold medications, some herbal remedies, such as licorice, and some recreational drugs such as cocaine and amphetamines.

In most cases, however, it is not exactly clear what causes high blood pressure. Could one or more of the root elements of the heart matrix play a role? I believe so. There are, however, many factors that are known to raise your risk of developing hypertension.

The risk of developing high blood pressure increases with:
- Age
- Family history of high BP
- Lack of exercise
- Smoking
- Being overweight or obese
- Sleep deprivation
- Regular alcohol consumption
- High amounts of salt in food (especially for those who are salt-sensitive)

DIABETES

Diabetes occurs when your blood glucose (blood sugar) is high. Glucose is an important source of energy for the body and comes mainly from food. Insulin, a hormone made by the pancreas, helps the glucose in the blood get into the cells to be used for energy, thus maintaining homeostatic levels of glucose at all times. Insulin is an essential hormone we cannot live without that regulates the metabolism of carbohydrates, fats and proteins.

There are two types of diabetes: type 1 and type 2. Type 1 diabetes occurs when the body's immune system attacks the cells in the pancreas that make insulin. As a result, people with type 1 diabetes do not make insulin and need to take insulin every day to stay alive. Type 1 diabetes usually strikes children and young adults, and only accounts for 5-10% of diabetes in the adult population.[12] The other 90-95% of diabetes among American adults is of type 2,[12] which usually starts as **insulin resistance**, where cells in the body cannot use insulin properly. Imagine that every cell is like a small house with a door. The door has a lock and insulin is the key. When insulin unlocks the door, glucose can enter the house. Insulin resistance occurs when the key is available but does not fit properly in the lock.

Diabetes is a major risk factor for heart disease, and its rising prevalence is in large part driving the upward trend in cardiac deaths in the last few decades. According to the CDC, between 1990 and 2010 the number of people living with diabetes tripled and the number of new cases

---

12. Centers for Disease Control and Prevention. National Diabetes Statistics Report. 2020. Atlanta, GA: Centers for Disease Control and Prevention, U.S. Dept of Health and Human Services; 2020.

annually doubled. The most recent statistics report (2020) from the Centers for Disease Control and Prevention (CDC) reported 34 million Americans had diabetes in 2018 and 1.5 million Americans are diagnosed with diabetes every year.

Of even greater concern are the 85 million American adults (more than one in three) who have pre-diabetes,[12] where blood glucose is higher than normal but not high enough to be classified as type 2 diabetes. But don't let the "pre" fool you. Untreated, pre-diabetes turns into type 2 diabetes. And having pre-diabetes in and of itself puts you at risk for cardiovascular disease. Sadly, more than 90 percent of people with pre-diabetes don't even know they have it.[12] **Something has to be done about this epidemic because pre-diabetes and insulin resistance are completely reversible.**

OBESITY

Obesity is another global epidemic and a huge (no pun intended) risk factor for heart disease and early death. It is closely tied to diabetes. It is estimated that 80% of people with type 2 diabetes are obese at the time of diagnosis or have a history of obesity.[12] The link between the two conditions is so strong that Shape Up America! trade-marked the term **Diabesity**. I like the term because it tells me that, not only are these conditions closely associated, but they likely have the same root cause. In conventional medicine, doctors often label different conditions that occur at the same time as "co-morbidities." In functional medicine, we suspect that most "co-morbidities" have the same upstream root cause.

The statistics related to obesity are alarming.[13] Across the United States, 83 million (more than one in three) adults are obese, but about **130 million American adults are categorized as being obese or overweight.** More disturbing is the rise of obesity in children—one in six children (ages 2-19) is obese and one in eleven young children (ages 2-5!) is obese. These young children cannot even choose their own foods. This condition is inflicted upon them, putting them at risk for diabetes, high blood pressure, early heart disease and shortened lifespans. If this trend continues, the children of today will be the first generation to live shorter, less healthy lives than their parents.

---

13. Hales et al. CDC National Center for Health Statistics data brief. Prevalence of Obesity. October 2017.

SEDENTARY LIFESTYLE

Our modern culture has both greatly benefitted and suffered from the technological and digital revolutions. Americans spend most of their waking hours now sitting indoors, much of it in front of digital screens. According to the American Heart Association, sedentary jobs have increased 83 percent since 1950. Physically active jobs now make up less than 20 percent of the U.S. workforce, down from roughly half of jobs in 1960. Modern conveniences such as online shopping and food delivery make it possible to hardly ever leave your home. Research suggests that only 21 percent of adults are meeting the physical activity guidelines for both aerobic and muscle-strengthening activities[14], while less than 5 percent perform 30 minutes of physical activity every day.[15] And what about today's children? When I was a kid, children played outside after school until they were called in for dinner. A National Trust survey found that children today spend half the time their parents did playing outside, despite being encouraged by their parents to go outside.

Sitting (and screen-time) has become the new smoking of our generation, affecting multiple organs and systems in our bodies. Prolonged periods of inactivity appear to be the big problem. Even if you're doing 30 minutes of exercise per day, it matters what you do the other 23 and 1/2 hours of the day. From an evolutionary perspective, humans were designed to move throughout the day. This was essential to our survival as a species. Our bodies are not prepared for this

---

14. U.S. Department of Health and Human Services. Healthy People 2020.
15. U.S. Department of Agriculture. Dietary Guidelines for Americans 2010.

rapid shift from activity to inactivity, and now a **sedentary lifestyle has been linked to:**
- Obesity
- Diabetes
- Heart disease
- High cholesterol
- Stroke
- Metabolic syndrome
- Inflammation
- Certain cancers, including colon, breast and uterine cancers
- Osteoporosis
- Depression and Anxiety
- Premature Death

The more sedentary you are, the higher your health risks are. Extended periods of inactivity can reduce metabolism, impair the body's ability to control blood sugar levels (i.e., insulin resistance), regulate blood pressure and break down fat. You can see here how the risk factors for heart disease and other chronic conditions have similar root causes, like physical inactivity. Breaking up long periods of inactivity will greatly lower your risk. Simple ideas include standing up every hour and walking around the office or home (if you work from home), doing one minute of movement each hour such as raising your knees, jumping jacks, running in place or dancing. Who cares who's watching? Invite them to join you.

THE CHOLESTEROL MYTH

High cholesterol is a well-recognized risk factor. In fact, the classic message from conventional doctors is that high cholesterol causes heart disease. This is not entirely true. There is much more to the cholesterol story that I will share with you. It is true that cholesterol remains a key player in the atherosclerotic plaque, which is the buildup of fatty material, inflammatory cells and other substances (remember the volcano) in the coronary arteries. However, the cholesterol levels typically measured in blood tests are not an accurate reflection of your true cardiovascular risk.

Myth: High cholesterol is inherited and there is nothing you can do about it. Also, not true. The most common inherited form of high cholesterol, Familial Hypercholesterolemia, is actually pretty rare. And there is a lot you can do about it.

Truth: In general, high blood cholesterol levels typically result from a combination of genetic and environmental risk factors. **Lifestyle choices including diet, exercise and tobacco smoking strongly influence the amount of cholesterol in the blood.**

So, what exactly is cholesterol? It is a type of fat (also known as lipid) that is produced by the liver. But not all cholesterol is the same. If you've had your blood cholesterol checked (lipid profile) you may have noticed several types of cholesterol reported (LDL cholesterol, HDL cholesterol). What is actually being reported is not cholesterol itself but the protein structures that carry the cholesterol in the bloodstream—the lipoproteins. These lipoproteins exist because cholesterol itself cannot move about the bloodstream on its own (it is not water-soluble) without being attached to a carrier protein.

Low density lipoprotein (LDL), often referred to as the "bad" cholesterol is responsible for carrying cholesterol particles throughout the body. But not all LDL are the same. There are different types of LDL that are not routinely measured in a standard lipid profile. **The truth is that not all LDL is bad.**

These different types of LDL are categorized by size and density. They are classified as either small, dense LDL or large, buoyant LDL. **Studies show that people who have mostly small particles, called Pattern B, have up to a three times greater risk than people with mostly large LDL particles, called Pattern A.**[16]

Lipoprotein (a) is another type of LDL, the level of which is determined by your genetics. **High levels of Lipoprotein (a) have been identified as an independent risk factor for premature heart disease and stroke** and, in my opinion, should be measured if you or a family member have had a heart attack or stroke at an early age or without other known risk factors, including high cholesterol.

Another important consideration is the number of LDL particles (called LDL particle number, or LDL-p) which is also associated with higher risk of atherosclerosis. This is very different than the LDL concentration, or LDL-c that is measured on your standard lipid profile, which is an estimated number. You can have a normal LDL-c (and think you're safe) but high LDL-p and actually be at high risk for a cardiac event.

High density lipoprotein (HDL) is often referred to as the "good" cholesterol that picks up excess cholesterol and takes it back to your liver where it can be used or excreted. Again, this is not the whole picture. There are subtypes of HDL and not all HDL are the same. Some are protective and some are not.

---

16. Hennekens CH et al. Low-Density Lipoprotein Subclass Patterns and Risk of Myocardial Infarction. JAMA 1988; 260(13): 1917-1921

Myth: Dietary cholesterol in food increases blood cholesterol levels. Forty years ago, dietary guidelines recommended that Americans significantly reduce their intake of cholesterol as well as saturated fats. This began the yo-yo recommendations that drive most Americans crazy. Eggs are bad, eggs are good, eggs are bad.

Truth: The consumption of dietary cholesterol has very little impact on blood cholesterol levels in most people. **When it comes to cardiovascular risk, refined carbohydrates and sugar are the primary culprits!** Still, there are some people with a genetic tendency to raise blood cholesterol levels after eating high cholesterol foods.[17] These people are referred to as "hyperresponders." Even though dietary cholesterol raises LDL in these individuals, it does not seem to increase their risk of heart disease. This is probably because the increase in LDL reflects an increase in the large, buoyant particles (Pattern A) and there is a concomitant rise in HDL, thus the ratio of LDL to HDL remains the same. This underscores the importance of the pattern as compared to LDL number alone.

Myth: Cholesterol is bad for your body.

Truth: Cholesterol is vital to the to the proper functioning of our bodies. It is involved in the following processes:

- Builds the cell membranes of every cell in your body
- Precursor to many hormones such as cortisol, testosterone, estrogen, adrenal hormones
- Essential for the production of vitamin D
- Produces bile acids, which help the body digest fat and absorb important nutrients

Another important type of lipid (fat) that is reported on a standard lipid profile is the triglycerides. When you eat, your body converts extra calories it doesn't need—especially

---

17. Clifton PM et al. Genetic control of response to dietary fat and cholesterol. World Rev. Nutr. Diet. 80:1-14

from carbohydrates—into triglycerides that are stored in your fat cells. Having a high level of triglycerides in your blood can increase your risk of heart disease. Extremely high triglycerides can also cause acute inflammation of the pancreas (pancreatitis).

High triglycerides are often a sign of other conditions that increase your risk of heart disease and stroke, such as Metabolic Syndrome and obesity. Metabolic Syndrome is an important cluster of conditions associated with increased risk of cardiovascular disease and includes:

- Increased waist circumference (too much fat around the waist)
- High blood pressure
- High blood sugar
- Low HDL
- High triglycerides

People who have 3 or more of these conditions are considered to have Metabolic Syndrome, which puts them at higher risk for heart disease and diabetes.

Dietary triglycerides are the fats we eat. But interestingly, consumption of excess carbohydrates, especially refined sugars and fructose also significantly (if not more so) raise the triglyceride levels in your blood.

The Truth is:
- Cholesterol and fats in general are vital to the proper functioning of your body.
- To better understand your individual risk, it is important to know more than the numbers provided on a standard lipid profile. Ask your doctor about particle numbers and particle size.
- What you eat and how you live determine your cholesterol and triglyceride levels and your cardiovascular risk.

In my practice, I routinely recommend an Advanced Lipid Profile which provides direct measurements of the different lipids, particle numbers, size and density. Based on each person's history and family history, additional tests may be ordered to get an even better idea of hidden risk factors lurking among the lipids. **One of these undesirables is oxidized LDL (ox-LDL)**. As the name implies, it is LDL that has been damaged by the process of oxidative stress. More on oxidative stress in the next chapter, but suffice it to say, that **ox-LDL is one of the biggest players in the initiation of the atherosclerotic plaque.** It is why small LDL are more dangerous—because they are more likely to be oxidized. It is generally the small LDL that can makes its way from the bloodstream into the artery, where it is oxidized and contributes to the atherosclerotic plaque.

PART III.THE HEART MATRIX

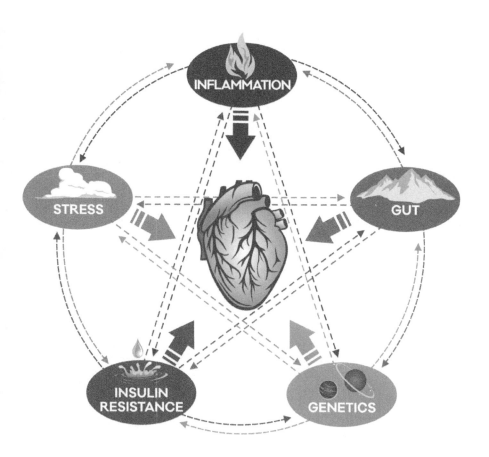

INFLAMMATION

Yes, cholesterol, particularly LDL cholesterol, is a major player in the atherosclerotic plaque. Yet, even with intensive lowering of LDL, cardiac events happen. In fact, information from the Get With the Guidelines database showed that up to half of all patients hospitalized with coronary artery disease have normal cholesterol levels.[18] This would suggest that something else is responsible for these events. The two root elements, Inflammation and Oxidative Stress, may explain the missing link.

Believe it or not, inflammation is a good thing, much like stress that we'll look at in the next section. **These response and recovery systems exist in our bodies to protect us.** Inflammation is part of the body's natural immune response to injury and infection, and is crucial to the healing process. When we are injured or infected, our immune system, i.e., acute inflammation, becomes activated and sends immune cells (monocytes, macrophages, T-cells) and other important mediators to that site to initiate the healing process. The word "in-flamed" should bring to mind fire, and in fact, its roots come from the Latin word inflammare, or to set on fire.

Chronic inflammation, on the other hand, is like that forest fire that never goes out. It is not only dangerous to your heart, but it is also implicated as the root cause of most chronic illnesses, including diabetes, autoimmune diseases and even cancer. Chronic inflammation may result from several circumstances. For example, if the body is unable to eliminate an agent

---

18. Sachdeva A et al for the Get With the Guidelines Steering Committee and Hospitals. Lipid Levels in Patients Hospitalized with Coronary Artery Disease: an Analysis of 136,905 Hospitalizations in Get With the Guidelines. Am Heart J 2009; 157(1): 111-117,e2

that sparks inflammation, such as certain food products like gluten or dairy, inflammation persists. Chronic inflammation may also result from exposure to chronic environmental toxins (including cigarette smoke), autoimmune disorders, chronic infections, insulin resistance and chronic stress (emotional, physical or dietary). If you recall the heart matrix and the root elements, inflammation and stress (especially oxidative stress) often coexist and spur each other on.

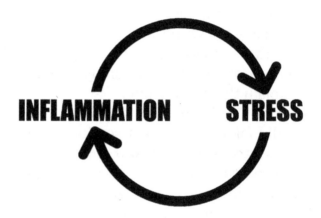

INFLAMMATION   STRESS

Inflammation can and does cause chronic stress, and stress causes inflammation. There seems to be a causal relationship between inflammation and oxidative stress that is perpetuated in a vicious cycle.[19] Chicken or egg, doesn't matter. They both essentially coexist and work together to create havoc in our bodies when one or both are out of balance.

So what is the role of inflammation in heart disease? Isn't heart disease a disease of high cholesterol building up in the heart arteries until it blocks blood flow to the heart, resulting in a heart attack?

19. Karbach S, Wenzel P, Waisman A, Munzel T, Daiber A. eNOS uncoupling in cardiovascular diseases--the role of oxidative stress and inflammation. Curr Pharm Des 2014; 20: 3579-94.

The truth is: **Heart disease is an inflammatory disease.** It sur-
prises me that despite decades of knowing that a heart attack is
an inflammatory process, most cardiologists are not addressing
chronic inflammation as a major risk factor. This is in large part
due to the non-existence (at least today) of an anti-inflammatory drug (other than statins) that can halt or reverse the process. Many pharmaceutical companies are in fact working on
developing just such a drug that will no doubt be overpriced and
may have associated side effects. Unfortunately, conventional
medical practices ignore readily available treatment options
that we will discuss in great detail later in the book.

Atherosclerosis—the clogging or hardening of arteries
has for centuries been thought to be the "cause" of coronary
heart disease. The hardening of the arteries is the result of,
not the cause of, coronary artery disease (CAD). CAD begins
and continues as inflammation. There is now clear evidence
that inflammatory cells are present in each and every step
of atherosclerosis from its early development to heart attack
and sudden death. For some time now, we have known that
inflammation plays a pivotal role in the occurrence of a heart
attack. Myocardial infarctions (MI) or heart attacks occur
when a plaque (volcano) ruptures into the lumen of the artery,
recruiting blood-clotting cells (such as platelets) and other
mediators that block blood flow completely with a blood
clot. It is inflammation at the fragile cap (volcano crater) that
causes the rupture, recruiting even more inflammatory cells
and chemicals to the site.

**But what is the role of inflammation in the earlier stages
of coronary artery disease?**

A large, randomized controlled trial published in the New
England Journal of Medicine in 2008, called the JUPITER trial,
shed some bright light on the major role inflammation plays.
In this global trial of apparently healthy men and women with
normal LDL but elevated levels of high sensitivity C reactive

protein (hsCRP), a marker of inflammation, treatment with a statin was associated with a significant reduction of major cardiac events, including death.

While bringing inflammation to the foreground was valuable to our understanding of coronary artery disease, the reaction by the medical community was to prescribe more statins, which is unfortunate. The "relative" risk reduction noted in the study translates to a much lower "absolute" risk reduction which means that the number of people needed to treat to prevent one cardiac event in relatively healthy people is about 500. This is a large number when you consider the safety and cost of taking a statin.[20]

Before jumping to treatment, we need to look upstream to find the root cause and its mechanism. Although we may refer to the blood vessels of the cardiovascular system as the plumbing, the vessels of the body, including the coronary arteries, are not stiff conduits for the flow of blood but are quite dynamic structures with many diverse functions.

Current wisdom now recognizes that atherosclerosis begins in the **endothelium. Injury to the endothelium and endothelial dysfunction are the earliest signs of atherosclerosis.** The endothelium is a highly active entity producing many factors (most notably nitric oxide) that regulate vascular tone, barrier function, inhibit platelet aggregation, oxidative stress and inflammation.

Endothelial dysfunction appears to be the result of excessive oxidative stress and inflammation, two of the five root causes of heart disease. In the presence of endothelial dysfunction, the usual protective functions of the endothelium are impaired and overtaken by increased permeability of the endothelium to LDL and inflammatory cells (monocytes and T cells) and decreased nitric oxide production.

The monocytes and their mature counterparts, the

---

20. Kelley, ME et al. JUPITER: a few words of caution. Circ Cardiovasc Qual Outcomes. 2009. 2(3) 286-288

macrophages, take up LDL ("bad" cholesterol) and attract more LDL to create the beginnings of the atherosclerotic plaque. The inflammatory cells, now in the intima of the artery, release more inflammatory chemicals and reactive oxygen species (ROS), oxidizing LDL and perpetuating oxidative stress. The reduction in nitric oxide, which normally keeps the vessel dilated and free of clotting agents, results in constriction of the vessel and recruitment of pro-clotting factors (platelets).

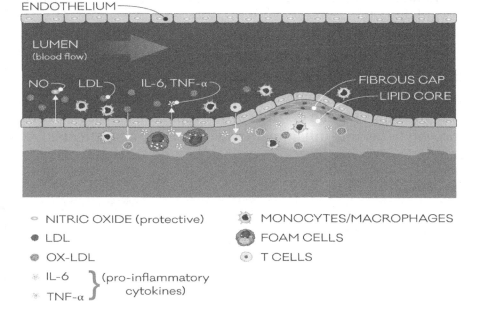

Atherosclerotic plaque progression. Normal endothelial cells produce nitric oxide which is cardioprotective. Endothelial dysfunction permits LDL cholesterol and immune cells (monocytes) to enter the arterial wall. LDL is oxidized to ox-LDL. Monocytes from the bloodstream enter the intima. Within the intima they transform to macrophages. By intaking ox-LDL macrophages form foam cells which produce pro-inflammatory chemicals called cytokines.

Endothelial dysfunction has been reported in relation to all of the risk factors for heart disease, such as smoking, diabetes, cholesterol, hypertension, obesity, physical inactivity and aging, all likely linked to the same root causes . . . oxidative stress and inflammation.

What are potential causes of chronic inflammation?
- Chronic infection (for example, periodontitis and dysbiosis)
- Autoimmune disorders, such as Rheumatoid Arthritis
- Smoking
- Pollutants, Toxins
- Obesity
- Chronic stress
- SUGAR
- TRANS FATS - now banned by the FDA
- Refined Carbohydrates, Gluten, and Dairy in susceptible individuals

The good news is that chronic inflammation is reversible and preventable. We'll talk more about ways to reverse and prevent inflammation in the Lifestyle chapter. There are simple things we can do and certain foods we can eat that are proven to be anti-inflammatory without any side effects.

STRESS

"It is not stress that kills us, it is our reaction to it."
~Hans Selye

Stress is finally being recognized as the major risk factor that it is. The role of stress in heart disease (and probably all chronic diseases) cannot be underestimated. Stress is such a pervasive problem in modern society that there is now an American Institute of Stress (AIS). The institute was founded in 1978 at the request of Dr. Hans Selye to provide information to the general public about the effects of stress on health and illness. According to the AIS, an estimated 75 to 90 percent of all doctor visits are for stress-related issues.

A brief explanation of the Stress Response is important to understand what happens when it goes awry and leads to disease. The stress response is an evolutionary adaptation which functions to protect all vertebrates from impending danger, preparing them to fight or flee for survival. Vertebrates are all beings with a spinal column including fish, birds, lions and human beings. The stress response begins in the primitive brain. While our brains have evolved to suit our environment, the primitive brain is that part of the brain that we share with all vertebrates, large and small. When danger or a threat is PERCEIVED, a signal is activated in the hypothalamus (command center) of the brain. The hypothalamus then activates 2 pathways that are responsible for the manifestations of the stress response in our bodies. These pathways are known as the **Sympathetic Nervous System (SNS)** and the **Hypothalamic-Pituitary-Adrenal System (HPA)**. Activation of SNS and HPA systems leads to release of adrenaline, noradrenaline and cortisol.

Every cell in our bodies is influenced by adrenaline, noradrenaline and cortisol.

To illustrate the Stress Response, imagine a lion and a zebra.

Zebras have eyes on the sides of their heads, so they usually will spot an oncoming lion with their excellent peripheral vision. This activates the Stress Response and prepares the zebra for flight (as fighting the lion would probably not end well). The stress response activates the release of adrenaline and noradrenaline, which results in increased heart rate, increased blood pressure and increased cardiac output (increasing blood flow), increased lung capacity, increased blood flow to muscles (for running) and decreased blood flow to the digestive and reproductive organs (not needed in the moment). The release of the hormone cortisol by the adrenal gland results in increased blood glucose release (for energy) and activation of the immune system (for repair of any injuries). If the zebra manages to outrun the lion, then the brain activates the **Relaxation Response,** which is mediated by the **Parasympathetic Nervous System, PNS (via the Vagus Nerve**), which restores all bodily functions to equilibrium.

The problem that has evolved in humans is that the

Stress Response is either repeatedly or chronically turned on when we "perceive" a threat. We use this same survival mechanism in response to events that, although trying and upsetting, are far less dangerous.

<u>The major sources of human stress are</u>:
- **Emotional**
- **Physical Pain**
- **Inflammation and Oxidative stress**
- **Dietary**

Emotional stress is the most common and results from your perception of an event, which can be a very dramatic event such as the loss of a loved one or a natural disaster. But, emotional stress can also be triggered by daily worries such as work, family, relationships and financial concerns. The human maladaptation to the Stress Response results in its chronic activation triggered by our emotions and our ability to ruminate over past events and ponder future events. We play those scenes over and over again in our minds, maybe thinking how it could have gone differently and worry about the future. Hans Selye calls these triggers "Stressors" and "Stress" our perception and reaction (physical, mental and emotional) to these triggers.

An important type of "stress" to be aware of is **oxidative stress.** Scientific evidence suggests that oxidative stress contributes to many chronic conditions, including heart disease. In fact, I believe that oxidative stress is one of the root causes of atherosclerosis. But what is oxidative stress, and what can we do about it?

Oxidation (the production of free radicals) and anti-oxidation are natural physiologic events that occur during normal cellular function. Normal cellular function results in the production of some free radicals. Free radicals are unstable molecules that can possibly damage DNA, cells, tissues and organs. Oxidative stress is an imbalance of this system (in favor of free radicals) at the cellular level.

Our amazing bodies naturally produce several antioxidants but also rely on the consumption of antioxidants, such as vitamins and minerals found in fruits and vegetables, to support our detoxification systems which neutralize the free radicals. Mild oxidative stress is not always harmful, and in fact, some studies suggest that free radicals play an important role in regulating detoxification and inflammation. **It is long-term oxidative stress or significant imbalance in favor of the free radicals that appears to result in cellular damage that is associated with aging and chronic diseases.**

As previously mentioned, oxidative stress can cause chronic inflammation, and inflammation can cause oxidative stress, creating a vicious cycle. **Several factors that you have some control over may increase your risk of oxidative stress.** These factors can include (and mimic the list for inflammation):

• Diets high in sugar and processed foods
• Smoking
• Obesity
• Alcohol consumption
• Pollution
• Exposure to radiation
• Exposure to pesticides or industrial chemicals
• Chronic (emotional) stress

Dietary stress occurs secondary to our bodies' response to the foods we eat. Then, in a vicious cycle, emotional stress often leads to a craving and consumption of "comfort foods" which are usually high in saturated fats and sugars. These foods can be pro-inflammatory and produce free radicals, contributing to oxidative stress.

Whatever the trigger, chronic stress leads to chronic activation of the sympathetic nervous system and release of adrenaline, noradrenaline, and cortisol (which can lead to high blood pressure), chronic stimulation of the heart (which can lead to heart failure), high blood glucose levels (which leads to insulin resistance and diabetes), increased fat storage and immune system dysfunction. It also leads to gut and reproductive dysfunction and is a major reason for infertility. With so many potential sources of "stress", it is no wonder that chronic stress is responsible for so many, if not all, chronic conditions today. Later on in the book, I will share some suggestions to manage stress.

The first step is in recognizing that it is our perception and our lifestyles that create our stress. The second step is to stimulate the all-important vagus nerve, which activates the Relaxation Response, the Parasympathetic Nervous System. The vagus nerve gets its name from the Latin, *"vagus nervus"*, meaning wandering nerve. It travels in a bidirectional fashion between the brain and the rest of the body, including the heart, lungs and abdomen. Stimulation of the vagus nerve through deep breathing will bring about a relaxed state.

INSULIN RESISTANCE

The hormone insulin is one of the most important hormones produced in our bodies. In fact, we cannot live without it, which is why type 1 diabetics (who cannot produce sufficient insulin) are dependent on insulin pumps or injections. Almost everyone knows that insulin is involved in the regulation of blood glucose, or blood sugar, which is absolutely true. But insulin also has many other functions throughout the body. Consequently, derangements in insulin function have widespread and devastating effects on many organs.

Insulin is a gene expression modulator which influences all of the following:
- Glucose Regulation
- Protein Metabolism
- Fat Mobilization
- Mitochondrial function (Energy Production)
- Inflammation
- Oxidative Stress
- Endothelial Function
- Lipid (Fat) Metabolism
- Sex Hormone Metabolism

Its main function is the regulation of our energy supply. As humans, we get our energy (our fuel) from the breakdown of the three macronutrients in our diet—carbohydrates, proteins and fats. Insulin plays an important role in the metabolism of all three nutrients. Consumed carbohydrates are broken down in the gut into glucose. Glucose is the main source of fuel used by cells.

Insulin is produced by the pancreas predominantly in response to elevated levels of circulating blood glucose after a meal including carbohydrates. Insulin then binds to insulin receptors on cells throughout the body to draw glucose into the cells from the bloodstream. As glucose moves inside the cells, blood glucose levels drop to normal and insulin secretion slows down. Excess glucose not used for immediate energy is stored in the liver or muscle as glycogen or in fatty tissue as fat (triglycerides).

When levels of glucose get low, the pancreas produces another hormone called glucagon, which signals the liver to release the stored glucose or make new glucose. This process, when working normally, ensures glucose levels that are never too high or too low.

Diabetes is a disease of insufficient or impaired insulin. There are two types of diabetes: type 1 and type 2. Type 1 diabetes occurs when the body's immune system attacks the cells in the pancreas that make insulin. As a result, people with type 1 diabetes do not make sufficient insulin and need to take insulin every day to stay alive. Type 1 diabetes usually strikes children and young adults, and only accounts for a small percentage of diabetes in the adult population. Most American adults with diabetes have type 2, which usually starts as **insulin resistance** where cells in the body cannot use insulin properly.

Insulin resistance, or impaired insulin sensitivity, occurs when circulating insulin is not easily recognized by certain cells. Think of cells as little houses with a front door. The door has a lock, which is the insulin receptor, and insulin is the key. Insulin resistance occurs when the key does not fit in the lock or can't turn the lock. This results in persistently elevated levels of blood glucose, and since the cells haven't received the energy they require (glucose), they send out signals to the pancreas to make more insulin. Now you have high glucose and high insulin circulating in the bloodstream until the pancreas ultimately burns out and can no longer keep up with the body's needs for insulin, leading to diabetes.

Many studies suggest that insulin resistance can occur

as a result of excess body fat.[21] Adipose (fat) tissues secrete a number of pro-inflammatory cytokines (molecular messengers), such as Interleukin 6 (IL-6) and Tumor Necrosis Factor-alpha (TNFα), which are associated with increased insulin resistance. IL-6 and TNFα impair insulin signaling. **Other factors that may contribute to the development of insulin resistance include lack of exercise, smoking and poor quality sleep. The link between these lifestyle factors and insulin resistance is most likely inflammation and oxidative stress.**

Insulin resistance, I believe, is one of the five root elements of the heart matrix. There is definitely an association between insulin resistance and heart disease, hypertension, and dyslipidemia. Significant scientific effort is underway to elucidate the underlying mechanisms. But what is known is that the vascular endothelium, heart, muscle, fat tissue, and liver are dependent on insulin to carry out many of their cellular functions, and thus impairment of insulin sensitivity appears to be upstream of many chronic conditions.

From a cardiac perspective, insulin is involved in several key functions of the vascular endothelial cells, largely mediated through its effect on nitric oxide (NO). Nitric oxide produced by the endothelial cells is responsible for keeping the vessels relaxed and clot free. Within endothelial cells, insulin normally exerts an anti-inflammatory effect and suppresses oxidative stress. Insulin resistance is strongly associated with endothelial dysfunction.

Insulin also plays a role in normal lipid (fat) metabolism. **Excess fat, which has been linked to insulin resistance, secretes inflammatory chemicals, TNF□ and IL-6, which not only impair insulin signaling, but also play a role in the breakdown of fat and endothelial function. Along with insulin resistance, we see increased inflammation, oxidative**

21. Wilcox G et al. Insulin and insulin resistance. Clin Biochem Rev. 2005; 26(2): 19-39

stress and high triglycerides, all of which increase cardio-vascular risk. IL-6 production is also enhanced by stress via the activation of the Sympathetic Nervous System (SNS).

Interestingly, cortisol, the stress hormone, and insulin have a counter-regulatory relationship. Cortisol enhances the production of glucose by the liver and by the breakdown of protein and it also makes fat and muscle cells resistant to the action of insulin. Under normal conditions, cortisol counter-balances the action of insulin. However, **with chronic stress, excess cortisol may contribute to insulin resistance.** And as we know, chronic stress is associated with increased inflammation, which has also been linked to insulin resistance. Once again, we see the interwoven relationship between the root elements of the heart matrix—Stress, Inflammation, and Insulin Resistance; they almost always exist together because they spur each other on.

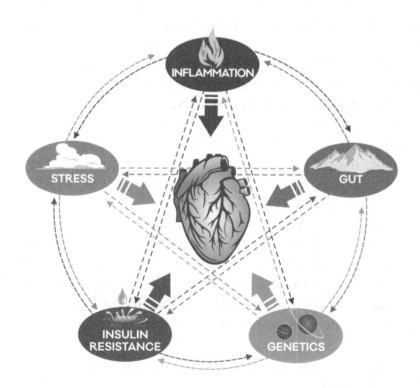

The good news is that insulin resistance is reversible through lifestyle interventions.

- **Weight loss**, especially loss of visceral fat, the fat around the waistline. As discussed above, excess fat cells secrete pro-inflammatory cytokines that impair insulin sensitivity. Studies have shown that weight loss results in improved insulin sensitivity.

- **Physical Activity/Exercise.** Skeletal muscles account for 60-70 percent of insulin-stimulated glucose uptake and thus are incredibly important in the regulation of blood glucose levels. Studies consistently show that exercise improves insulin sensitivity although the mechanism is not as of yet fully understood.

- **Decrease consumption of Carbohydrates (carbs).** Some studies suggest that a low-carb diet (with or without high fats) can reverse insulin resistance and improve insulin sensitivity. This makes sense because if you are eating fewer carbs that get digested into glucose, there is less demand for insulin.

But remember that **not all carbs are the same**. Some carbohydrates, like vegetables, are important for proper cellular function. Dietary carbohydrates refer to sugars, starches and fibers that we consume. **Fiber is key to good health and one of the reasons why all carbs should not be eliminated from our diets.** Carbohydrates are often classified into simple carbs (such as glucose and fructose) and complex carbs. Simple carbs are sugars that can easily and quickly be used for energy, often leading to a faster rise in blood sugar and insulin. Complex carbs, having a more complex chemical structure, generally take longer to digest with a slower rise in blood sugar. The problem with this scheme is that there are good simple carbs like fruits, rich in vitamins, minerals and antioxidants and bad simple carbs like candy, and there are many good complex carbs like vegetables, legumes and whole grains and bad complex carbs like refined sugars in white bread and pasta which contain mostly starch but little fiber or other beneficial nutrients.

Another way of categorizing carbohydrates is the **glycemic index.** The glycemic index ranks carbs on a scale from 0 to 100 based on how much they raise blood sugar levels after eating. Foods with a high glycemic index (GI) like white bread, are rapidly digested and cause substantial fluctuations in blood sugar. Foods with a low GI are digested more slowly, prompting a more gradual rise in blood sugar.

Personally, **I prefer the classification of "whole" vs "refined" carbs.** Whole carbs are real foods (vegetables, fruit, legumes and whole grains) that are unprocessed and contain all their natural fiber and nutrients. Refined carbs have been stripped of all nutrients. So, **as a general rule, if it's a whole food in its natural, fiber-rich state, it is healthy.** If you have insulin resistance, eating low carb meals with less than 100-130 grams of carbs per day (depending on the individual) can be effective in improving insulin sensitivity and weight loss.

- **Eat plenty of fiber**, predominantly soluble fiber from plants. This super nutrient slows the absorption of glucose in the gut, which evens out blood sugar levels. I recommend trying to consume at least 25-40 grams of fiber a day. The recommended amount varies with age and gender. Currently, dietary fiber intake among American adults is about 15 grams a day. Eat more fruit, vegetables, beans, seeds and nuts.

- **Intermittent Fasting.** Many studies suggest that intermittent fasting can improve insulin sensitivity. During these fasting periods, insulin is not in demand. This gives the pancreas a break and the cells an opportunity to recover and become more insulin sensitive.

- **Sleep Well.** Good sleep is critical to normal biological function. It is the time when all the systems repair and restore and is characterized by decreased glucose turnover. Studies suggest that short duration sleep (less than 6 hours) increases your risk of insulin resistance and diabetes. Extending your sleep by one hour may improve insulin sensitivity.

GENETICS

"Your genes are not your fate"
~Dr. Dean Ornish

One of the greatest accomplishments of the 21st century was the mapping of the human genome. The word genome refers to all of the genes (DNA) in our cells. Think of the genome as the blueprint or instructional manual for the development and function of a human being. The Human Genome Project reported that there are approximately 20,000-25,000 human genes found in our 23 chromosomes, far fewer than was anticipated given the complexity of human nature. This raises the intriguing question of what else plays a role in our human expression? The Human Genome Project has laid the foundation for researchers to unravel many of our medical mysteries.

It has also become apparent that most chronic diseases, including heart disease, are attributable to both genetic and environmental influences. Many believe that the environment, everything that we are exposed to in our lives, may play a more important role. Our environmental exposure (which includes absolutely everything we're exposed to from birth to death, such as food, pollutants, etc.) and our biological response is called the **Exposome**.

The mapping of the human genome also allowed the identification of more than 3 million genetic variations called SNPs - single nucleotide polymorphisms. **SNPS (pronounced "snips")** occur normally throughout a person's DNA and are often found commonly in unrelated individuals. They are now being used to study and identify the predisposition to certain traits, response to certain foods and drugs, susceptibility to toxins and risk of developing certain diseases such as heart disease.

It is well established that several cardiac diseases are inheritable and disease-causing genes have been identified for many of them, including several inherited arrhythmias and cardiomyopathies (diseases of the heart muscle). However, genetic studies of coronary artery disease initially lagged behind these other types of heart disease, but new technology in genetic testing is now starting to uncover some very exciting discoveries. I believe the reason genetic studies of CAD lagged behind other cardiovascular disorders is precisely because of the complex nature of the disease, which is caused by many genetic factors, environmental factors AND the interactions among these factors.

Among the many conventional CAD risk factors, a family history of heart disease (particularly at an early age) is one of the most significant independent risk factors. Just how CAD is inherited from parents, meaning which genes and what pattern of transmission, is still largely unknown. But exciting advances are now being made in identifying disease-causing genes and susceptibility genes for CAD. **This has tremendous implications for personalized medicine.**

An example of the utility of genetic testing for specific cardiac disorders is the identification of genetic mutations in individuals with Long QT Syndrome, an inherited syndrome associated with fatal arrhythmias linked to sudden cardiac death. Patients with one of the known mutations respond to a certain medication, while patients with another known mutation in the same gene respond to a completely different therapy. You can see how important it is to know which mutation is involved as these patients are at risk for sudden cardiac death.

Several genes and SNPs have been identified and are being studied in association with coronary artery disease. For example, the gene MEF2A was reported as a causative mutation in a large single family affected by CAD in Scandinavia.[22] However, subsequent studies in other pop-

22. Wang Q. Mutation of MEF2A in an inherited disorder with features of coronary artery disease. Science. 2003; 302:1578-1581

ulations have found mixed results with regard to causality. More studies with larger samples are needed and, I suspect, underway. Interestingly, this gene encodes a protein that is highly expressed in the endothelium, again pointing to the important role of the endothelium in the early stages of CAD.

In 2007, a series of associated SNPS called, 9p21, were identified.[23] **9p21 SNP increases the risk of CAD.** This gene is very common, occurring in 75 percent of the Caucasian and Asian population, with 50% inheriting a single copy of the gene variant and 25% inheriting 2 copies. In the overall population, having one copy of the variant is associated with a 20-25 percent increased risk and having 2 copies (one from each parent) is associated with a 40-50 percent increased risk of CAD. **The most revelatory finding is that the increased risk associated with 9p21 is independent of any of the conventional risk factors.**

Another common gene influencing cardiovascular risk is the APOE gene. This gene is one of the most common genes affecting LDL cholesterol and codes for the protein apolipoprotein E. The **APOE gene has been associated with an increased risk of high LDL, Coronary Artery Disease, and Alzheimers disease.**

There are at least 3 variations (called alleles) of the APOE gene(E2, E3, and E4) and thus six possible heritable combinations (one from each parent) which determines your genotype—E2/E2, E2/E3, E3/E3, E3/E4, E2/E4, and E4/E4. The E2 allele is the rarest form with the lowest risk for CAD and E3 is the most common form. **The APOE4 genotype, found in approximately 25 percent of the population, carries a higher risk of CAD and Alzheimers.** An interesting finding is that although having higher LDL cholesterol levels and higher risk for CAD, individuals with the E4 genotype have less reduction in response to statin therapy (statins being the

23. Roberts R. Genetics of CAD: An Update. Methodist Debakey Cardiovascular J 2014 (1): 7-14

primary treatment for high cholesterol). Similar genetic variability to popular cardiac medications have been found with other SNPs.

Now there are at least 50 SNPs linked to CAD. Of these 50, how they confer increased risk, the mechanism, is yet unknown. **There is however some evidence that several of these genetic risk variants predispose to CAD through inflammatory pathways.** The identification of CAD susceptibility genes and SNPs is undoubtedly remarkable and valuable information and will likely change how cardiology is practiced in the near future.

Genetic testing is available and recommended for some of the heritable heart diseases, particularly if there is a family history of disease, for example Long QT syndrome, Hypertrophic Cardiomyopathy or Familial Hypercholesterolemia (FH). Coronary artery disease, however, is more complex than heredity alone. **The discovery of 9p21 (and other CAD genetic markers) has led to a growing interest in using genetic testing to predict individuals at risk for the development of CAD.** There are currently only a few laboratories that offer a panel of SNPs. The panels including several CAD SNPs should greatly improve predictability. Early identification of genetic risk creates the potential for aggressive personalized preventive measures. The ultimate goal of genetic testing (or any predictive test) is to improve upon the prediction of CAD conferred by standard risk factor assessment. And, in fact, studies have shown that incorporating 9p21 gene to standard risk assessments improves prediction of CAD.

Even more exciting is the interaction of our genes with our diet, our Exposome. Compared with APOE3 and E4, APOE2 genotypes have reduced CAD risk but a propensity for increased triglycerides, insulin resistance and obesity. These individuals do well with a diet low in carbohydrates and high in heart-healthy fats. In contrast, individuals with APOE4, with its effect on cholesterol and fat metabolism, do not process dietary fats and alcohol well. These individuals should aim for low fat intake and consider not drinking alcohol at all. Doing this may significantly decrease your risk of CAD and Alzheimer's. Another interesting study suggested there may be an interaction between the 9p21 SNP and consumption of vegetables and wine, pointing again to environmental influence.

New genetic discoveries are occurring at a rapid pace. Yet, there still remains some cautious skepticism regarding the clinical utility of genetic testing in the general population. Bear in mind that much is still unknown in this burgeoning field of molecular genetics, especially with regards to coronary artery disease. A "negative" genetic test does not exclude the possibility of having heart disease nor does it exclude the possibility of an as-yet undiscovered genetic process in an individual with coronary artery disease. According to Dr. Robert Roberts, one of the world's foremost experts in molecular cardiology, *"The role of genetic risk factors in the management of CAD is yet to be determined. Since many of them are independent of known risk factors, genetic risk will, in the future, have to be incorporated in the guidelines."* At present, genetic testing is not covered by most insurance providers.

Remember identification of a SNP is not a diagnosis of heart disease; it is associated with increased susceptibility to CAD and/or heart attack. **Given the increased predictive value, not only for CAD, but response to medical therapy and certain diets, I do believe, in many cases, it can help guide doctors and individuals in decision making regarding the benefits of further cardiac testing and aggressive lifestyle modifications.**

As enlightening as your genetics may be, your genes are not your destiny. Epigenetics is a field that describes molecular modifications known to alter the activity of genes without changing their DNA sequence. These modifications are induced by environmental factors.

Epigenetics is the influence of our environment and our lifestyle on the expression of our DNA. In essence, epigenetic changes can turn off "bad" genes and turn on protective genes through these modifications. Interestingly, your parents' and your grand-parents' epigenetics can also be inherited. That means that you may have inherited and been born with their dietary and environmental exposures as well. To me, this emphasizes the importance of a detailed family history when gathering information from a patient.

Lifestyle factors associated with Epigenetics
- Diet
- Obesity
- Atmosphere (pollution)
- Smoking
- Physical Inactivity
- Alcohol
- Chronic Stress
- Social, cultural and economic circumstances

Does this list look familiar? It is the same list responsible for inflammation and stress!

Remember, your genes are not your destiny. Information is power. Having this information gives you the opportunity to choose a lifestyle that can completely alter your fate. Armed with the knowledge of your genetic and environmental risk factors (i.e., lifestyle), aggressive lifestyle modifications and medications where needed can be used to delay or prevent coronary artery disease.

THE GUT-HEART CONNECTION

"All disease begins in the gut."
~Hippocrates

The old saying, "the way to someone's heart is through their stomach" could very well be true. Studies show that gut health and heart health are intricately linked, and the key to a healthy heart may be in your gut.

By now, most people have heard something about the gut microbiome. But what exactly is it, and what does it have to do with your heart? The human genome is a term used to describe all our genes. **The microbiome is used to describe all the genes from the ' lions of diverse micro-organisms (bacteria, viruses ar gi) that live in and on our bodies.** One of the sur the Human Genome Project was the discovery th .uman genome only contains about 20,000-25,00(ɔ, and the microbiome may be hundreds of times larɡ ɹe truth is that we have ten times as many microbial cei ɔ as human cells. Take a moment to think about that. We are not entirely "human" beings. We often think of bacteria and viruses as unwanted invaders. But these micro-organisms (when functioning normally) are critical to our good health. We are nothing more than a biological ecosystem—a community of organisms living together, co-dependent on each other for survival.

We rely on the microbiota to perform many important functions that we cannot perform ourselves. **The microbiota digest and extract nutrients from food (like fiber), make certain vitamins, metabolize drugs, detoxify carcinogens, stimulate renewal of cells in the gut lining, play a role in the gut's barrier function, and play a pivotal role in our immune systems. Our microbiome also influences our** human genome—a perfect example of Epigenetics.

Research on the gut microbiome is proliferating at a rate that is not easy to keep up with. Also challenging to keep up with are all the new terms. For the purposes of this book, the microbiome is the collective genome of the microbes. **Microbiota refers to the composition of the varying organisms.** The majority of the microbiota reside within our intestines. Once again, "balance" is the key word. A happy, healthy gut microbiome consists of a certain balance of diverse organisms, which varies from one individual to the next. Another keyword is diversity. The richer and more diverse the community of gut microbes, the healthier the microbiome. **Many environmental factors play a role in regulating the composition and function of the gut microbiota. Studies have shown that diet and lifestyle are important factors.** Any alteration of the normal microbiome is termed "**dysbiosis**".

So, what does this have to do with your heart?

Well, it turns out that there is a complex interplay between the microbes in our intestines and most of the systems in our bodies, including the cardiovascular system, as well as the nervous system, endocrine system and immune system. As I've alluded to in the Heart Matrix, all of these systems are interconnected to each other and to the heart. Imbalances in these systems lead to stress, inflammation, insulin resistance and epigenetic phenomena which also influence the gut microbiome. **Dysbiosis has been implicated as the cause of inflammation, insulin resistance, oxidative stress, and epigenetic regulation.** Again, we can see how dysfunction in one system can wreak havoc on all the systems and increase the risk of heart disease. There goes that vicious cycle again!

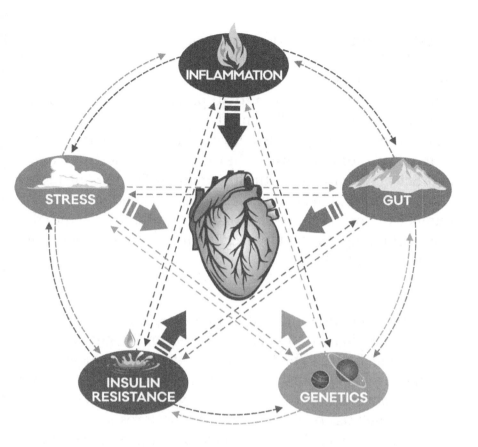

Factors the can result in dysbiosis include:
- Diets high in sugar or processed foods
- Medications, such as antibiotics and proton pump inhibitors (PPIs)
- Poor dental hygiene
- High levels of stress, depression or anxiety

There are three potential mechanisms by which dysbiosis can lead to cardiovascular disease. Further research is underway to better define these links, but here is what we know so far.

1. **SIBO** - small intestinal bacterial overgrowth
Everything in nature has its place. The microorganisms in the gut also have their place predominantly in the large

intestine. Certain conditions can lead to migration and over-growth of bacteria from the large intestine into the small intestine. This is known as a condition called SIBO. SIBO is found in many cases of (up to 80 percent) of irritable bowel syndrome (IBS), but I will admit that it was surprising to me to learn of the significant link between SIBO and heart disease.

In a 2018 study published in the journal *Digestive Disease and Sciences*, patients with SIBO had an 80 percent higher chance of having heart disease.[24] They also had an increased number of coronary arteries that were affected. To me, this was frightening, especially after I found out that at one point in my life I had SIBO.

2. TMAO

Another potential mechanism involves the metabolism of certain proteins we consume. When certain gut microbes use choline, found in high quantities in eggs, red meat, poultry and fish, they can produce trimethylamine (TMA). TMA is then converted in the liver to trimethylamine N-oxide or TMAO, which has been linked to atherosclerosis.

In a review published in the *Journal of the American Heart Association*, 19 studies confirmed a link between elevated TMAO levels and increased risk of heart disease. People who had higher levels were 62 percent more likely to have heart disease.[25] High TMAO levels have also been linked to higher mortality rates, independent of other commonly linked risks such as diabetes and obesity. These findings suggest that evaluating serum levels of TMAO may be reasonable when evaluating someone's risk of cardiovascular disease, particularly amongst individuals who consume the precursors of TMAO.

24. Shen B. Association Between Small Intestinal Bacterial Overgrowth by Glucose Breath Test and Coronary Artery Disease. Digestive Disease and Sciences. 2018. 63(20; 412-421

25. Qi L. Gut Microbiota Metabolites and Risk of Major Adverse Cardiovascular Disease Events and Death: A Systemic Review and Meta-Analysis of Prospective Studies. J Am Heart Assoc 2017: 6(7)

3. LEAKY GUT

The microbiome plays a key role in the barrier function of your intestinal lining. When that gut lining is disrupted, it becomes permeable or "leaky." **A leaky gut allows food particles and bacteria to migrate into the cells and subsequently into the bloodstream, where it activates an inflammatory cascade.** This is especially problematic when there are lipopolysaccharides (LPS) present. LPS is an endotoxin (a toxin that is present in the cell membranes of certain bacteria) which have been shown to be pro-inflammatory.

Another interesting tidbit is that certain gut microbes have literally been found within the artery plaques of patients with heart disease. For years, scientists have been unable to figure out how they got there. One plausible hypothesis involves the leaky gut, allowing certain microbes to enter the bloodstream and relocate in artery walls. This area of interest is in need of more research.

As previously mentioned, the gut microbiota perform many protective functions. Another potential mechanism linked to heart health is the production of important short chain fatty acids. **Short-chain fatty acids (SCFA) are produced by the gut microbiome from undigested carbohydrates such as fiber.** These SCFA may be involved in blood pressure regulation along with improved glucose metabolism, lipid metabolism, and insulin sensitivity.[26]

The bottom line is that this information takes "you are what you eat" to a whole new level. Not only do we have to think about what we feed ourselves, but what are we feeding our microbiota. The food choices we make each and every day have a significant influence in determining the health of our microbiota. How can we support our microbiota that exist to support us?

---

26. Chamber ES et al. 2018. Role of Gut Microbiota-Generated Short-Chain Fatty Acids in Metabolic and Cardiovascular Health. Current Nutrition Reports. 7(4); 198-206

Well, we know that balance and diversity are key to a happy, healthy microbiome. The richer and more diverse the microbiota, the lower your risk of diseases associated with dysbiosis, such as heart disease. **Eating foods high in fiber and antioxidants support and fuel the microbiota**. Eat a variety of high fiber vegetables such as artichokes, leeks, onions and garlic. These types of fiber are considered prebiotics. Some people may benefit from adding a probiotic food or supplement. Probiotics are beneficial microorganisms that are taken in an attempt to restore balance and diversity of the gut microbiota. This can be accomplished with fermented foods like yogurt, sauerkraut or kimchi.

Just as important as what you eat, is what you should avoid. Steer clear of artificial sweeteners like aspartame, sucralose and saccharine. These disrupt the metabolism of microbes and reduce diversity. As much as possible, avoid unnecessary antibiotics. Antibiotics destroy both good and bad microbes, including your good gut microbes.

Exercise your microbiota. Regular physical activity is not only good for your heart, it is good for your gut, too. Many of the lifestyle ideas I will share in the next few chapters have also been found, like exercise, to support the microbiome. Before we look at lifestyle, you may want to know what your personal risk is for the development of heart disease.

PART IV. DETECT AND PREVENT

"Prevention is better than cure."
~Desiderius Erasmus

Now that you know all the important risk factors and root causes of heart disease, it is time to determine your individual risk and keep your risk low forever. **The more risk factors you have and the greater the severity of each risk factor, the higher your chance of developing coronary artery disease.** According to the CDC, half of all Americans have at least one modifiable risk factor. The sooner you identify and modify your risk factors, the better your chance of preventing heart disease. The following suggestions are only for those individuals without any known heart disease.

A simple starting point is to **know your "basic numbers."** These include:

- Blood pressure
- Cholesterol (total cholesterol, LDL, HDL and triglycerides)
- Blood glucose (and Hb A1C)
- BMI (body mass index) and WC (waist circumference)

Optimal numbers for health are:
- Blood pressure less than or equal to 120/80 mm Hg
- Total cholesterol less than 200 mg/dl
- LDL cholesterol less than 100 or less than 70 if you have CAD or diabetes
- HDL cholesterol greater than 40 in men, 50 in women
- Triglycerides less than 150 mg/dl
- Fasting blood glucose less than 100 mg/dl
- Hb A1c less than 6%
- BMI less than 25

You may notice that several of the risk factors I've described in this book are not listed here.

Cardiovascular risk is traditionally calculated (literally) using one of several scoring systems, such as the Framingham Risk Score, Reynolds Risk Score or the ASCVD (Atherosclerotic Cardiovascular Disease) Risk Algorithm from the joint AHA (American Heart Association)/ACC (American College of Cardiology) taskforce. All of these algorithms attempt to determine your risk of developing heart disease or having a stroke in the next 10 years. Unfortunately, all risk-estimation scores have several inherent limitations. These population-based scores use different risk factors and prediction endpoints (coronary artery disease vs cardiovascular disease), and there is wide variation in predictions when compared to each other. Studies have also shown overestimations and underestimations of risk with these algorithms.[27]

How do these cardiac risk calculators work? For each risk factor, you get points, the points are plugged into an algorithm (or equation) and voila—your predicted "risk." The scores can be useful in identifying individuals with cardiac risk factors and should be the start of a conversation about lifestyle modification, not the end of a conversation. If you use any of these calculators and your estimated risk is greater than 5%, I urge you to talk to your doctor.

In conventional medicine, once identified as having anything greater than borderline to intermediate risk, the primary focus turns to identifying individuals who are eligible for statin therapy. Statins are among the most commonly prescribed drugs in the United States. Much of the focus in conventional risk assessment is around lowering cholesterol.

Statin medications do lower cholesterol and have been associated with reduction in cardiovascular events and death.

---

27. Ridker P et al. Comparison of the Framingham and Reynold Risk Scores for Global Cardiovascular Risk Prediction in the Multiethnic Women's Health Initiative. Circulation. 2010; 125(14): 1748-1756

This is true. However, they do not benefit everyone who meets these criteria, and furthermore, they are associated with side effects that are not insignificant, and there may be risks associated with cholesterol that is too low. That is why a personalized approach is the only way to go.

There are several cardiac risk calculators available to both physicians and the public. They all vary slightly. Some include diabetes, some don't. Some include ethnicity, some don't. Their predicted outcomes are also somewhat different.

The ASCVD Risk Calculator, a widely used calculator, was developed in support of the 2013 AHA/ACC primary prevention guidelines. **The following risk factors are used to estimate your 10-year risk of developing heart disease.**

- Age
- Diabetes
- Sex
- Race
- Smoker
- Total cholesterol
- HDL cholesterol
- Systolic blood pressure
- Treatment for hypertension

These algorithms, however, do not identify everyone at risk for heart disease. A large, observational study from the National Registry of Myocardial Infarction (heart attack) during the years 1994-2006 found that 15 percent of first-time heart attack patients had no traditional risk factors. Furthermore, mortality was greatest in those patients without any traditional risk factors.[28] It is also well established that cardiovascular events continue to occur in patients

---

28. Greenland P et al. Number of Coronary artery disease Risk factors and mortality in Patients with first Myocardial infarction. JAMA 2011: 306(19); 2120-2127

with "normal" cholesterol levels on statins. The same can be extrapolated to the other traditional risk factors. Thus, having a strategy to reduce only the traditional risk factors is not adequate.

The Functional Medicine approach is to go upstream of the traditional risk factors to the root causes. It is highly likely that inflammation, insulin resistance, stress, alterations in gut microbiome and epigenetics play a role. Going even further upstream, we look for the underlying cause of these dysfunctions, which are almost always found in the lifestyle, genetics and environment.

The most recent updated guidelines by the joint AHA/ACC task force for the primary prevention of cardiovascular disease was published in 2018. The good news is that they emphasize that **"A comprehensive patient-centered approach that addresses all aspects of a patient's lifestyle habits and estimated risk of a future ASCVD event is the first step in deciding on where there may be a need for pharmacotherapy."** The guidelines now also encourage a team approach with shared decision making between clinician and patient. This is fantastic.

Unfortunately, the goal remains focused on identifying individuals that should be prescribed a statin drug for primary prevention. This is particularly problematic when the standard lipid profile used for assessing cholesterol is not that useful a predictor of risk. Standard lipid profiles are missing a lot. In fact, more than half of all heart attacks occur in people with normal cholesterol levels.[29]

Treatment guidelines for cholesterol reduction are focused entirely on LDL cholesterol, which is calculated from the standard lipid panel. It turns out that total cholesterol and the calculated LDL (LDL-C) numbers are pretty useless.

---

29. Fonarow GC et al. Lipid levels in patients hospitalized with coronary artery disease: an analysis of 136,905 hospitalizations in Get With the Guidelines. Am Heart J. 2009: 157(1);111-117

The number of LDL particles (LDL-P) and LDL size are more strongly associated with risk than LDL-C. Studies show that people who have mostly small, dense particles (Pattern B) have up to three times greater risk than people with mostly large particles (Pattern A). This makes sense because the small molecules can penetrate the endothelial cells of the coronary arteries more easily and wreak their havoc in the walls of the arteries, leading to plaque formation.

The new guidelines now suggest that, "In adults at border-line risk or intermediate risk, it is reasonable to use risk-enhancing factors to guide decision making regarding statin therapy." Some of these **"Risk Enhancers"** are:

- Family history of premature heart disease
- Metabolic Syndrome
- Inflammatory disease
- If measured:
  ◦ Elevated hs CRP (marker of inflammation)
  ◦ Abnormal lipid biomarkers

If there is still uncertainty, further testing with Coronary Artery Calcium (CAC) measurement to document subclinical disease is reasonable.

The truth is that most doctors will plug your information into the calculator, and if your risk is determined to be anything greater than low (5 percent), a statin will likely be recommended. You will be advised on lifestyle modifications, but as to the team approach and shared decision making, I have my doubts. Shared decision making may be as simple as asking you, "Do you understand?" As for advanced testing for other risk factors, it is rarely done and rarely covered by insurance.

If you are like most of my patients, this may not sit well with you. My patients don't want to know what their "relative risk" is for the next 10 years; they want to know what their individual risk is and if their risk is high; knowing that heart disease can be silent, they want to know if they have silent disease.

Despite the abundance of data implicating inflammation in the development and progression of coronary artery disease, the American Heart Association and the American College of Cardiology do not recommend the routine screening for vascular inflammation. **Looking for inflammation can detect patients at risk BEFORE the development of traditional risk factors and heart disease.** Similarly, with insulin resistance, identifying patients with IR before the development of diabetes or even pre-diabetes can significantly lower rates of heart disease. This is what Functional Medicine doctors describe as the "upstream" approach.

Depending on the individual, I may recommend some of the following tests to better identify and monitor cardiac risk, particularly in patients with established heart disease, diabetes, high blood pressure, metabolic syndrome, high cholesterol (on standard lipid profile), obesity, family history of heart disease and individuals with an estimated ASCVD risk greater than 5 percent:

- Advanced lipid testing (LDL-p, LDL size)
- Markers of vascular inflammation
- Insulin Resistance panel
- CIMT (Carotid Intima Media Thickness)
- CAC (Coronary Artery Calcium)
- Genetic testing

Carotid Intimal Medial Thickness (CIMT) is a noninvasive ultrasound of the carotid artery in your neck, which measures the thickness of the innermost layers of the artery. This measurement identifies plaque build-up and inflammation in the carotid arteries, which has been consistently correlated with coronary artery disease and stroke.

Coronary Artery Calcium (CAC) scoring, also known as a Heart Scan, is a noninvasive CT scan of the heart. The scan measures the amount of calcified plaque (which is made up of fat, cholesterol, calcium and inflammatory cells) in the coronary arteries. Your score is an excellent predictor of your likelihood of having heart disease or a heart attack.

The procedure itself takes only a few minutes but does involve radiation. The amount of radiation exposure is about the same as 10 x-rays.

Based on these results, along with personal history and preference, my patients and I discuss various options for preventing or reversing heart disease. The remainder of this book will go into some of these options in more detail. While every treatment program is unique and tailored to each individual, first line treatment is always lifestyle modifications. That being said, as a cardiologist who has taken care of thousands of patients with severe heart disease, I have no problem recommending statins (and do) when necessary. However, we know that lifestyle changes alone (if fully embraced) can prevent the development of heart disease and can even reverse disease in those who have it. In the landmark trial, the Lifestyle Heart Trial, Dr. Dean Ornish demonstrated that individuals with coronary artery disease who followed his intensive lifestyle program had regression of atherosclerosis (plaque) without any medications![30] Imagine what a healthy lifestyle could do to prevent disease.

---

30. Ornish D. Lifestyle Heart Trial. 1998 and 2002

PART V. LIFESTYLE MEDICINE

"Your lifestyle—how you live, eat, emote, and think—determines your health. To prevent disease, you may have to change how you live."
~Brian Carter

So now we get to the fun stuff. Transforming our lives and taking control of our health and the health of our loved ones by taking a close look at how we live. Our 'lifestyle' is everything that we do, from brushing our teeth in the morning to what we do before going to sleep. **Making some small changes in our lifestyle can have profound effects not just on how you feel physically, but research suggests that making lifestyle changes makes you happier.** And we've all experienced how happiness tends to have a ripple effect in all areas of our life with our jobs, friends and family. Some studies even show that happiness can prolong our lifespans, which is only great if you're healthy.[31]

There's no right way to change your lifestyle—everyone is different with different likes, dislikes, cultural norms and values. What works for one person may not resonate for someone else, which is why I practice personalized medicine. But one thing is certain—the key to your health and happiness is YOU. And what you put into it is what you get out of it. We put so much time and energy on making other people happy—our bosses, our significant others, our parents, our kids and our social media friends (LOL) that we don't always take the time for self-care.

---

31. Kubzansky LD et al. Optimism is Associated with Exceptional Longevity in 2 Epidemiologic Cohorts of Men and Women, PProc Natl Acad Sci USA, 116(37): 18357-18362

For many of us, we have this preconceived notion that a healthy lifestyle is boring, restrictive or punitive. I think I live a pretty healthy lifestyle, and I will tell you that my life is anything but boring or restrictive. I love to eat and eat what I want most of the time. Luckily what I want is usually healthy. My palate has adapted to healthy foods and yours can, too. Now don't get me wrong, I live in New York City with some of the best restaurants in the world, and my favorite food is pasta. So every once in a while, I eat it without any guilt and enjoy it far more than if I were to eat it every day. I recently discovered, however, after eating more pasta than I should, that I had SIBO (small intestinal bacterial overgrowth) and the best diet for healing my gut was a low FODMAP diet, which meant, among other things, gluten free. At the time I was struggling with abdominal discomfort, weight gain, acne, muscle pain and fatigue. I wanted to feel better, so I adhered to the required change in my diet and . . . Shazam . . . everything got better and I didn't feel deprived. I learned new recipes and discovered new favorite foods. And now I can enjoy pasta every once in a while.

Remember that lifestyle change is not all about diet. Sadly, the word diet has taken on a derogatory meaning—that of a temporary, restrictive way of eating after which you go back to your old habits. This idea of diet is almost always doomed to fail. The word <u>diet</u> has its origin in the Greek language, meaning "way of living." That is how I like to think of the word diet for myself and my patients. But because of the negative association, I try not to use the word diet and instead talk about nutrition or eating styles.

Lifestyle, more than just how we eat, involves how we fill our days and how we interact with each other—how we work, play and sleep. It also involves how we think and respond to the stressors of the world.

If you think about it, **lifestyle is all about choice. You have the freedom and the power to choose the best "way of living" for yourself and your loved ones.** What follows in this section of the book are general recommendations for you to consider and hopefully choose to incorporate into your life. A doctor cannot tell you how to live. I know from personal experience that telling my cardiac patients who've already suffered a heart attack to eat heart healthy, exercise and don't smoke often fell on deaf ears. Many patients, after a frightening heart attack, feel a loss of control, and so they maintain that control through their lifestyle choices. During the course of my career, I've learned that telling people what to do is useless. I now give them back control and information and allow them to choose their path without guilt or shame.

Information is Power. I believe that many of the poor lifestyle choices are based on misinformation. In the modern healthcare model (which is really disease care), healthcare providers are not discussing lifestyle and its impact. In a model where doctors spend 15 minutes with a patient, after discussing medications and side effects, there is little time left to address lifestyle. The system also does not incentivize physicians to spend their time discussing lifestyle with patients. Their compensation, sadly, is based on the number of patients seen and procedures done. The good news is that I do believe that there is—there has to be—a shift towards patient-centered quality care, which has as its greater goal the prevention of chronic diseases like heart disease.

More than 80 percent of chronic conditions, including heart disease could be avoided by adopting a healthy lifestyle.[32] Numerous well-designed studies show that a healthy lifestyle can prevent or treat high blood pressure, diabetes, high cholesterol, heart disease, depression and dementia. On top of that, it's practically free and has no bad side effects. As a matter of fact, it's only side effects are improved sleep, increased energy and weight loss.

I believe any lifestyle change has to be meaningful and pleasurable. What gives your life meaning? What motivates you to do and be your best? Is it health, wealth, family time, play time? What gives you pleasure? **The secret to successful**

lifestyle change is finding the joy in your choices. If you value time with your family or friends, continue to enjoy time with them but maybe choose a healthy activity over a sedentary one. Time with my friends is incredibly valuable to me. My friends and I love to cook (and eat), so we get together and whip up some delicious healthy meals. We also go for walks or runs together, which gives us the opportunity to connect on a different level.

I want to share with you, in the next few pages, more information about the power of lifestyle changes and a few suggestions that may resonate with you. Start where you are and take small steps. It is not my intention that you do everything all at once. Studies suggest that taking small steps is more effective and sustainable. You have to walk before you can run—literally.

THE FOOD CONUNDRUM - WHAT TO EAT

"Let food be your medicine and medicine be your food."
~Hippocrates

Why is what we eat so important for our heart health? It begins with the gut-heart connection. Food is much more than just calories and energy. **Food is medicine.** Let me clarify by sharing one of my favorite quotes:

"The food you eat can be either the safest and most powerful form of medicine or the slowest form of poison."
~Ann Wigmore

Good foods are foods that are rich in nutrients (vitamins, minerals, antioxidants and phytochemicals). These nutrients have medicinal powers, and our ancestors have known this for thousands of years. **Food is also information.** Food can indirectly alter our gene expression (nutritional epigenetics) through our microbiome.

Alterations in our gut microbiome can lead to leaky gut, which can lead to systemic inflammation, Insulin Resistance and increased fat deposition (obesity). So, what alters our gut microbiome? Studies suggest that food modifies the intestinal microbiome. The impact can be beneficial or detrimental, depending on what we eat and how that affects the makeup and number of the different bacterial populations in our gut. For example, diets rich in protein have been associated with increased beneficial bacteria. Whereas diets high in sugar, refined sugars and saturated fats alter the microbiome in a negative way.

Looking at the heart matrix again, we can see that genetics and epigenetics play a role in the health of our microbiome and vice versa. There is no one-diet-fits-all approach that works. We are all genetically different with different micro-biomes, and different individuals may process the same food differently. Our genetics play a role in shaping the microbiome, and certain gut bacteria can alter our immunity through epigenetic modifications. The future of personalized medicine may well incorporate genetic information about individual metabolic responses to meals. However, we are not there yet, and the best we can do is learn from the science we have so far. And the science suggests that diets high in sugar and saturated or trans fats have a negative impact on the microbiome leading to inflammation and a host of other chronic diseases. So, what are you going to do with this information?

Making good choices when it comes to food can seem daunting. Many people are confused about what constitutes healthy foods. Mass confusion is not surprising given the overwhelming, often contradictory misinformation we are exposed to from the food industry, policy makers and even healthcare providers. The influence of the food industry via multiple media outlets is almost inescapable, and they are succeeding in brainwashing Americans to eat foods that are completely void of nutrition. And what about all the diet trends? Should we eat low fat, high fat, low carb, high carb, high protein? **How can we be expected to make good decisions when the so-called experts debate what is the best diet themselves?**

Understandably, many people turn to their doctors for advice. The truth is, however, that most doctors are not adequately trained in nutrition. When I went to medical school, very little time was allotted for nutrition education. To my knowledge, this trend has not changed very much in the last 30 years. When I became interested in lifestyle medicine, I studied nutrition on my own, and now nutritional counseling is one of the primary tools of Functional Medicine that I use every day in my practice.

Other roadblocks to eating healthy include the misconceptions about the cost and effort required to prepare and cook meals at home. I was fortunate that while growing up, although my mother worked part-time, on the days she was home, she prepared home-cooked meals for the rest of the week, except Fridays—pizza night. I remember sitting in the kitchen with my mom doing my homework, and then as I got older, she taught me to cook quick, simple meals.

Meal preparation is one of the greatest diet hacks I know. Most people want to provide their family with healthy meals, but often feel they don't have the time to cook. The truth is that it doesn't take that much time. Shopping and cooking with your family members goes beyond the nutritional value of the meal. Time together is priceless, especially when you've all played a part in putting it together. It beats going to a fast food restaurant for a "happy meal" that is making your bodies very sad. It's about exposure—what we expose ourselves and loved ones to. Again, I was fortunate. I never went to McDonald's as a child, and we didn't have candy in the house except after Halloween, so I never craved these kinds of food. If you don't expose your children to it, chances are they won't miss it.

One thing is for certain: the Standard American Diet is S.A.D. And the good news is that experts DO agree on what constitutes a healthy diet. They may debate the "style" of eating (a little bit more of this or a little bit more of that), but not the basic principles of nutrition for the purpose of disease prevention. For example, one expert may recommend a Paleo diet while another recommends a Mediterranean diet. These are just labels with minor differences. **The consensus is that a healthy diet is a whole-food, plant-rich diet, the only style of eating that has been scientifically shown to prevent and reverse chronic diseases like heart disease and type 2 diabetes.**

What is whole food? Real food in its natural state. This means that food hasn't been refined, tampered with, or processed. The food is fully intact with all of its own vitamins, minerals and other micronutrients. It's the difference between an orange and orange juice in a box. Your health is determined by the quantity and quality of nutrients consumed (vitamins, minerals, fiber and phytochemicals) in your food. We need to place less emphasis on the macronutrients (carbohydrates, fats and proteins) and be more mindful of the micronutrients. Only 12 percent of US food consumption is plant food (USDA Economic Research Service, 2009), and up to half of this consumption may be processed, for example, almonds in candy bars, apples in apple pies, or consumed as french fries, and of course these would not be healthy choices. According to U.S. Department of Agriculture estimates, roughly 60 percent of America's calories come from refined and processed foods (such as soft drinks and packaged foods) and 25 percent comes from animal-based foods.

There's a good reason that the standard American diet is SAD. The standard American diet leads to standard (chronic) American diseases that lead to standard American deaths. In my opinion, it is the primary cause of the obesity and diabetes epidemics. The good news is that, armed with this information, we have the power to make better choices.

Here are some basic principles to consider for your nutritional lifestyle. Note that I don't recommend counting calories or a specific breakdown of macronutrients (proteins, fats and carbs) for everyone. Based on our genetics and our environment, our metabolism and metabolic needs differ. That being said, these are principles that everyone can begin with to create a healthier life.

1. Eat real whole-food at every meal.

2. Enjoy Mother Nature's gift to us—plants. More than half your plate should be filled with vegetables at every meal. But you don't want to eat the same veggies every day. First of all, you will likely get bored very quickly. Second of all, variety is not only the spice of life, it matters when it comes to eating vegetables. Eating veggies in a rainbow of colors provides more of the vital nutrients that we need. Remember that veggies are carbs, but they are the good carbs. However, I suggest limiting the starchier veggies because they may cause a spike in your blood sugar and insulin levels. Better choices are non-starchy veggies such as artichokes, asparagus, broccoli, leafy greens, peppers, mushrooms, squash, tomatoes, eggplant and many more delicious veggies that support your blood sugar levels and are high in fiber. Consuming foods high in fiber can lower high blood pressure and high cholesterol and has been positively linked with heart health.

3. Avoid sugar. Sugar is Enemy #1. Sugar, particularly refined carbohydrates such as anything made from white flour (bread, pasta, cereals, muffins, donuts, cookies, etc.) spike your blood sugar levels and increase insulin production, which as we now know, is associated with Metabolic Syndrome, Diabetes, Obesity, Inflammation and Heart Disease. Many of my patients ask about fruits. While it is true that the simple sugars found in fruits can spike blood sugar levels, they are also incredibly rich in powerful antioxidants and phytochemicals. So, I recommend consuming fruits that are considered low-glycemic such as berries, cherries, apples and peaches. Carbohydrates with a low glycemic index (GI) are more slowly digested, absorbed and metabolized and cause a lower and slower rise in blood sugar and therefore, usually, insulin levels.

4. Avoid processed and refined foods. You know what they are but to mention a few – soda, fruit juice, white bread, potato chips, pastries, cookies, candy and cakes.

5. Limit dairy. Cow's milk is meant for the nourishment and growth of calves (think growth hormones), not humans. Other great alternatives include unprocessed almond, cashew or oat milk.

6. Eat responsibly sourced protein such as grass-fed animals, farm raised poultry allowed to move freely and not pumped full of hormones and antibiotics and wild fish.

7. Eat good fats. Fats are an essential macronutrient, just like carbohydrates and proteins. They are essential for brain function, cellular structure, thermoregulation, hormone production and so much more. Good fats are monounsaturated fats (like avocado and olive oil) and polyunsaturated fats, such as omega-3 fatty acids found in some fishes (salmon, mackerel, anchovies, sardines, herring), nuts, and seeds (flax and chia). The key is moderation.

8. Eat legumes (lentils, peas, beans, chickpeas, soybeans and peanuts) in moderation.

9. Limit gluten. Many experts are getting behind the gluten-free trend that many people are adopting. For people with celiac disease, wheat allergy or gluten sensitivity, it makes sense to avoid gluten. Some experts suggest that gluten can damage the gut lining, even in patients without celiac disease. More research is needed before I can make a global recommendation that everyone should be gluten-free. Besides, if you're following principles #1 and #2 above, you're already avoiding many of the foods that contain gluten.

10. Most importantly, enjoy what you eat. Food is one of life's greatest pleasures and food is community. It brings family and friends together. The secret to a sustainable lifestyle change is to find the joy in it. And with food, I think it's easy to do. Experiment, try different foods, try different recipes, try one of the many food delivery options and share the experience of delicious health with those you love. And for dessert, don't forget the dark chocolate!

KEEP MOVING

"Take a discovery walk today to find what's missing in
your life. There's peace in the whisper of the wind, hope in the
sun smiling from the clouds, strength in every step forward. "
~Toni Sorenson

I purposely titled this section "movement" because I feared that had I titled it "exercise," many would skip over the chapter. And so I will jump to the punchline, **movement is medicine**. And exercise can be fun and should be fun. As I've mentioned before, for any sustainable lifestyle change, it has to be meaningful and pleasurable. Maybe we don't enjoy exercise because we've stopped playing as adults, but

"We do not stop playing because we grow old,
we grow old because we stop playing."
~Benjamin Franklin

And I would add to that we grow sick. Everybody knows that exercise is good for your health. Why is it then so dreaded? Americans spend most of their waking hours sitting—indoors. Research suggest that only 21 percent are meeting the physical activity guidelines set by the US Department of Health and Human Services (HHS), while less than 5 percent perform 30 minutes of physical activity per day. Sitting has become the new smoking.

I'm not going to ask you to exercise. I'm asking you to move and play and have fun. A prescription for fun doesn't sound so terrible, does it? Unfortunately, the word exercise brings to mind images of going to a gym, spending hours there on boring machines, surrounded by skinny people that don't look like you. You do not ever have to step inside a gym to exercise, which is defined as any activity requiring physical effort for the purpose of improving and sustaining health and fitness. And for the record, most gyms across the country do not fit that image. Non-exercise activities such as raking the leaves, mowing the lawn and climbing the stairs can burn significant calories, commonly referred to as the N.E.A.T. (Non-exercise activity thermogenesis) way to exercise.

Once again, I think information is power. If we know all the benefits of physical activity and how it works, maybe we can embrace it with open hearts. Let's start with the benefits. Studies show that

Physical activity can:
- Lower your blood pressure (and maybe your requirement for medications)
- Lower your blood glucose (and maybe your requirement for medication)
- Improve insulin sensitivity
- Lower your cholesterol
- Improve your metabolism
- Reduce your risk of heart disease
- Help you lose weight
- Help your mood (endorphins)
- Decrease depression and anxiety
- Improve your sexual health
- Improve brain function
- Improve immune system function
- Decrease inflammation
- Strengthen bones and muscles
- Improve your sleep
- Reduce your risk of some cancers
- Increase your chances of living longer

Impressive list, isn't it?

The HHS and American Heart Association recommend at least 150-300 minutes (2.5-5 hours) a week of moderate-intensity, or 75-150 minutes (1.25-2.5 hours) a week of vigorous-intensity aerobic physical activity. This time can be broken up any way you like doing anything you like. For example, you can walk 30 minutes a day five days a week or 15 minutes of vigorous walking or jogging five days a week.

You have to crawl before you can walk, and walk before you run. Acknowledge where you are and make your movement goal attainable, something that will easily fit into your daily routine. Carving out an hour for exercise every day may seem impossible for many people. I suggest beginning by moving for short periods of time several times throughout the day rather than the run and done strategy. This strategy removes the time obstacles so many people believe keep them from exercising. All you need is 10 minutes in the morning, at lunchtime and after dinner. I think this is doable for anyone. Once you get used to doing this and realize you enjoy it, increasing your time will come naturally. Personally, I try and start each day with a short yoga routine (set to my favorite yoga playlist) which gets the oxygen and the blood flowing and brings me into a state of equanimity and readiness for my day.

Walking is one of the most commonly prescribed forms of movement because it is easy and free and doable for most people.

If walking is not your thing, you can do anything that gets your blood flowing and your heat beating a bit faster—bike, swim, play tennis, play golf (but skip the cart), yoga, dance. Many people are turning to high intensity interval training, otherwise known as HIIT. These workouts consist of short bursts of high intensity effort followed by brief periods of rest. HIIT is becoming increasingly popular because the workouts are generally shorter in duration and studies suggest just as effective as moderate intensity continuous effort. Some studies suggest all you need is as little as 7 minutes of HIIT.

Whatever you decide to do, why not involve a friend, family member or coworker in your activities? One of my patients was concerned that her son was overweight, so she bought him a mini trampoline. Now they both jump together. Neither of them view this as exercise. Instead they are having fun and quality time together. Furry friends are also great companions and love to go out on walks. My own dog, Rocky, changed my life. He was a beautiful yellow Labrador retriever, full of energy, and loved to go out. And it wasn't enough for me to let him out in the backyard. He insisted I go with him and it didn't matter if it was raining or freezing, we went out and we enjoyed everything nature had to offer us. **Bottomline is move your body doing something you love and love what you do. The more you do, the greater the health benefits.**

In addition to aerobic exercise, strength training and flexibility are beneficial for your heart health. Strength training builds muscle mass and bone density. Again, you don't have to go to a gym and lift weights. You can keep a few weights or resistance bands at home, use home objects or just use your body weight. Flexibility is important to prevent pain and injury.

What are you willing to do?

"It always seems impossible until it is done."
~Nelson Mandela

STRESS MANAGEMENT - BUILDING RESILIENCE

"Stress is the trash of modern life - we all gen-
erate it, but if you don't dispose of it prop-
erly, it will pile up and overtake your life."
~Danzae Pace

The word stress that is so ingrained in our daily lives was coined by Dr. Hans Selye a little more than 50 years ago to describe how the body responds to different demands placed upon it. Who doesn't feel stressed these days? We live in a fast-paced, demanding world. Most of us would define stress as coming from our jobs, financial concerns, family, relationships, health or major life events. But Selye defines these demands as the stressors and our reaction as the stress. It is our reactions that result in the physiologic responses that is "stress." Our reactions also lead to our behaviors. Think about how you respond to what you perceive as overwhelming demands on your life. Do you get angry or upset? Do you overeat or drink more than you should? The response starts in our hearts and brains (our feelings, perceptions and thoughts) and affects every organ and every system in our bodies.

The role of stress in heart disease (and probably all chronic diseases) cannot be underestimated. Stress is such a pervasive problem that there is now an American Institute of Stress (AIS). The institute was founded in 1978 at the request of Dr. Hans Selye to provide information to the general public about the effects of stress on health and illness. According to the AIS, an estimated 75 to 90 percent of all doctor visits are for stress-related issues.

We learned earlier in the book that the stress response is an evolutionary survival mechanism designed to prepare us for imminent danger (fight or flight response). When our brains perceive a problem, a cascade of physical changes occur, mediated by the release of adrenaline and the hormone cortisol throughout the body. This results in revving up the heart and lungs and sending blood to the muscles (preparing the body to run) and decreasing blood flow to the gut and reproductive organs. As you recall, cortisol also increases blood glucose levels and activates the immune system, for energy and wound healing. Once the perceived threat is gone, your body is meant to return to a relaxed state of equilibrium. This is mediated by the parasympathetic nervous system (PNS).

Frankly, short bursts of acute stress can be beneficial in our lives—we learn how to cope with more difficult situations and we develop resilience. The problem and the implications for our health is when we respond to everyday stressors in a perpetual, ruminating fashion. The stress response, chronically "turned on," then results in high blood pressure, high heart rate, high blood glucose, high cholesterol, high insulin, weight gain, poor sleep and inflammation. As humans, though, we are not limited to fight or flight responses. The solution lies in recognizing what triggers these events and our response to those triggers.

The most common sources of stress triggers are emotional, dietary, physical and inflammatory or toxic, in that general order. Emotional stress is the biggest source and refers to your perception of an event. Examples of emotional stress include loss of a loved one, divorce, financial concerns, family concerns, relationships, health and political concerns. Dietary triggers occur secondary to blood sugar and insulin fluctuations in response to the foods we eat. Physical stress comes from pain. Inflammation from foods or infections and toxins from our environment can also trigger the stress response.

The good news is that, short of changing your circumstances, there are several wonderful ways to alter your stress response. Those daily stressors may never go away and, unfortunately, we may even be presented with a major stressor, such as illness or death of a loved one. We will continually be challenged to fight or flee and our bodies and our health pay the price. But we can learn how to control our responses and in turn significantly reduce our risk of disease. If stress, especially emotional stress, is PERCEIVED, then one may posit that we can alter our stress response by changing our perceptions.

> *"You can't always control what goes on outside,*
> *but you can always control what goes on inside."*
> ~Wayne Dyer

CHANGE THE NARRATIVE

It is more than lip service to suggest that we can change our thoughts, perceptions, attitudes and behaviors. Modern behavioral science agrees. Dr. Albert Ellis, creator of rational emotive behavior therapy (REBT) claimed that how people respond emotionally and behaviorally to an event is determined predominantly by their perception of the event, not the event itself. Perception is everything. How we think about and interpret a situation informs our attitudes, which determines our behaviors.

Cognitive reframing is a useful technique developed by Albert Ellis to control and change negative thoughts. Say, for example, that at your quarterly review with your boss, she tells you you've done a good job but she would like you to work on increasing sales. Your perception may be that she was displeased and you think you are not good at your job. This may evoke feelings of anxiety and stress. Using cognitive reframing, you take a breath and re-analyze the situation and your feelings and write them down. Write down the objective evidence that supports your thoughts, "Maybe my sales numbers can improve." Then write down objective evidence that contradicts the thought, "Overall, my boss was pleased with my work, and I am good at my job." With this more balanced view or perception of the situation, you're likely to find that you feel less anxious and stressed. By changing the narrative, we change the outcome.

There are many things in your life that you can't control, but there is so much you can control. You can decide who you share your life and energy with, how to spend your time and money. You can choose your words and tone of voice when you speak to others. You can choose what to eat, drink, watch on television and read. You can choose how you will respond to unfortunate situations when they arise, and whether you will see them as misfortune or opportunities for growth. And most importantly, you can control your thoughts and emotions.

Cognitive reframing is one of many possible strategies to reduce your stress. I will describe a few others that are supported by research and that I personally like. However, there isn't a one-size-fits-all option when it comes to stress relief. What works for one person might not work for another. I recommend trying different approaches and find what resonates best with you.

MEDITATION and MINDFULNESS

Meditation is simply the act of focused attention or concentration. Western medicine is finally validating what ancient yogis have known for thousands of years—that our minds, our perception of reality, is at the root cause of all suffering. The age-old practice of meditation is now growing in popularity as a stress reduction technique.

Meditation is Medicine. Research has confirmed a myriad of health benefits associated with the practice of meditation. These include stress reduction, decreased anxiety, decreased depression, improved memory and improved longevity.[2,3]

Thanks[32] to the marvels of modern medical technology, we now have objective evidence of the benefits of meditation. Neuroimaging (MRI, fMRI, and PET) studies have shown changes in both the function and structure of the brain during AND after meditation.[33] Scans performed on expert meditators elucidated the activation of brain networks involved in self-regulation, attention, perception and memory. MRI scans also showed an increase in the grey matter of the brain. That's right—the brain gets bigger with meditation. The changes at the brain level turn on the relaxation response, which improves cortisol levels, immune function, reduces blood pressure. **A recent pilot study in the *Journal of Nuclear Cardiology* showed that the addition of transcendental meditation (TM) to standard cardiac rehab for patients with coronary artery disease resulted in significantly increased blood flow to the heart** as measured using positron emission tomography (PET scan).[34] This was a small study but beaming with immense promise to directly measure the effect of meditation at the heart level. If that's not enough reason, meditation has been linked to slowing the aging process, with changes noted at the cellular level and at the brain level.

Despite its known benefits, meditation still seems elusive to many people, likely due to the many misconceptions about

32. Horowitz S Health benefits of meditation. Altern Complement There 2010; 16:223-2228

2. Burns JL, Lee RM, Brown LJ. The effect of meditation on self-reported measures of stress, anxiety, depression and perfectionism in a college population. J College Stud Pyschother. 2011; 25: 132-144

3. Ray IB, Menezes AR, Malur P, Hitbold AE, Reilly JP, Laie CJ. Meditation and coronary heart disease: A review of the current clinical evidence. Ochsner J. 2014; 14: 696-703

33. The meditative mind: A Comprehensive Meta-Analysis of MRI Studies; Biomed Res Int 2015

34. Nidich SI. Effects of cardiac rehabilitation with and without meditation on myocardial blood flow using quantitative positron emission tomography: A pilot study. Journal of Nuclear Cardiology 2019

meditation. Some may regard it as a religious practice, but the practice of meditation does not belong to any religion. Meditation means different things to different people, but in general, meditation is the act of focused concentration. That's it. This act of focused concentration, whether the focus be on your breath, an image, a sensation or a mantra, turns on the relaxation response. Many people think you have to sit on the floor in lotus position. This position is not accessible to most people. I suggest sitting in a chair, feet on the ground with a straight back (supported if need be). One of my yoga teachers would say, "A straight spine, a clear mind." That has stuck with me. So, no slouching please.

The object of focus is really up to you. Personally, I like the breath. Bring your attention to your breath. Follow the inhale in through your nostrils, to the chest, belly and the rest of your body and the exhale from the body out the nose. As you follow your breath, begin to slow the pace of your breath, breathing in for a slow count of four, breathing out for a slow count of four. Other objects of focus include images (sun, flame, flower, etc.) or a mantra. A mantra is a word or a sound which may or may not have any meaning that is repeated in your mind over and over again. The root of the word mantra comes from "man," meaning mind, and "tra," meaning tool. So mantra is a tool of the mind to help us focus. In yoga, we often repeat inspirational mantras, for example, "Om", "Om Namah Shivaya", or "Sa-ta-na-ma," that remind us of our own divinity. In Transcendental Meditation (TM), you are given a mantra by your instructor which has no specific meaning. Whatever the focus, understand that thoughts will pop up, and that is perfectly okay. In fact, it is part of the process, which ultimately creates the changes in our neural pathways. We become more aware of our thoughts, and we can redirect our attention.

Mindfulness is the practice of being fully present in the moment, aware of everything going on around you and inside you—your thoughts and feelings, without judgement.

Jon Kabat-Zinn, founder of MBSR (mindfulness-based stress reduction), says, "Mindfulness means paying attention in a particular way; on purpose, in the present moment, and non-judgmentally." Mindfulness meditation focuses on being aware or mindful of the present moment—your environment, sights, sounds, sensations and thoughts. Here again, the breath is important as an anchor to keep you in the moment, simply being mindful of our breath, without controlling it in anyway. Again, when the mind wanders, and it will wander, just notice, and redirect your awareness back to the breath, back to the moment. Mindfulness meditations invite thoughts into the practice, more as a matter of noticing that thoughts have occurred, not to judge or interpret the thoughts. One of my yoga teachers uses the imagery of a file cabinet. When the thoughts come in, label it "thought" and file it away in the cabinet.

If you are new to meditation, consider connecting with a meditation instructor or take a class at a meditation center or yoga studio. Programs such as TM and MBSR are formal training programs found just about anywhere. You can also find videos on YouTube, and there are wonderful apps that you can download onto your phone as well. **The beauty of mindfulness is that you can practice it anytime, anywhere. Start by being mindful of all the beauty around you.** My dog, Rocky, was my mindfulness teacher. When we would go out on walks, he would pause the moment he got out the door and the moment we hit the beach and take a breath in. He taught me to do the same—to smell the air, to listen to the waves crashing, the children playing, to feel the sand under my feet and the sun on my skin. Reconnecting to nature in a mindful way is one of the best stress busters I know. Then you feel empowered to take moments of mindfulness at work and at home—just taking notice of everything as it is, without judgment.

TAKE A BREATH

The breath is the link between the body and the mind. That is why it is used as a focal point in any form of meditation or stress management technique. Although breathing is an involuntary bodily function, how we breathe can be a sign of our stress levels. Have you ever noticed that you hold your breath when scared or anxious, or maybe your breath speeds up and becomes shallow? This is the breath under the influence of the sympathetic nervous system (fight or flight). Taking nice, slow, deep breaths in and out activates the parasympathetic nervous system (rest and relaxation) via stimulation of the vagus nerve. The vagus nerve then sends signals to the entire body, including heart, lungs, brain and gut, resulting in reduced heart rate, blood pressure and improved digestion. Recent studies suggest that breathing may act directly on the brain itself to influence emotions.[35]

YOGA

Yoga, an ancient practice dating back over five thousand years, has become increasingly popular in the West as a means to manage stress. Many people, myself included, are initially drawn to yoga for its physical benefits, improving flexibility. But we very quickly learn the secret medicine, which in Sanskrit is called the _chikitsa._ At first, you don't know what it is, you just know that you leave a yoga class feeling calm and peaceful, even if the class was a hot yoga or power yoga class.

There are many styles of yoga, such as Hatha, Ashtanga and Iyengar, but they all incorporate the same basic elements

---

35. Wackle K, Schwarz LA, Kam K, Sorokin JM, Huguenard JR, Feldman JL, Luo L, Krasnow MA. Breathing control center neurons that promote arousal in mice. Science 2017; 355: 1411-1415

of movement, body awareness, breath, linking breath to movement and meditation. The chikitsa is the union of mind, body, breath and spirit. Numerous randomized controlled trials have shown a reduction in blood pressure, cholesterol, inflammation and, here again, a slowing of the aging process with improved quality of life.

Yoga therapy utilizes the principles of yoga to personalize individual or small group practices with certain health needs or goals. All yoga styles and classes are not ideal for everyone, especially if there are any health concerns. As much as I love yoga, I have witnessed people doing poses they should not be doing and, unfortunately, not being properly guided by the teachers. Most yoga teachers have minimal training (200 hrs) and are not trained to deal with most medical issues. This need is what inspired me to study further and specialize in therapeutic yoga and cardiac yoga.

Cardiac yoga is yoga therapy for cardiac patients. Patients with cardiovascular disease, including coronary artery disease, high or low blood pressure, should always advise their yoga teachers about their conditions and ask for modifications. Cardiac yoga is now (slowly) being introduced into traditional cardiac rehab for patients who have been hospitalized with a heart attack or have undergone cardiac procedures, such as stent implantation or bypass surgery. These cardiac yoga classes often start seated in a chair where many of the traditional poses are modified. Chair yoga is also a great alternative for anyone with chronic pain, limited mobility, and some older adults. The chair is a great starting point where we can focus on breathwork and meditation. Using a chair doesn't necessarily mean that you are sitting the whole time. Based on physical ability, standing poses and ultimately transitioning to the floor are encouraged.

HEARTFULNESS

If you think about it, most of our stress reactions involve a "feeling"—perhaps of anxiety, frustration, irritation, rejection, overwhelm or anger. **The heart is where we experience our feelings, both negative and positive.** We now know that we can work with our feelings to reduce stress. **The heart and brain are intimately connected** in a variety of ways. The heart sends blood rich in oxygen and nutrients to the brain, and the brain sends information to the heart. Traditionally, however, it was thought that communication of information was one-way, from the brain to the heart via the autonomic nervous system (ANS). The sympathetic nervous system (SNS) revs up the heart (increase heart rate) and the parasympathetic nervous system (PNS) calms it down (slows heart rate). Relatively new research (in the last 50 years) has shown that the heart communicates to the brain in several ways: neurologically via nerve impulses, hormonally and energetically (rhythmically).[36]

Fascinating recent research has found that **the heart has a complex nervous system of its own, often referred to as the heart-brain,**[37] and in fact, the heart actually sends more signals to the brain than the brain sends to the heart. Even more fascinating (at least to me), is that **the signals from heart to brain affect how we perceive and respond to situations and events.** [38]

The input from the heart-brain is represented in the patterns of the heart's rhythm. Heart rate variability (HRV) is the variability in the length of time between 2 consecutive

---

36. Armour, JA. Anatomy and function of the intrathoracic neurons regulating the mammalian heart, in Reflex Control of the Circulation, IH Zucker and J.p. Gilmore, Editors, 1991, CRC Press: Boca Raton. p 1-37

37. Armour, JA, Potential clinical relevance of the 'little brain' on the mammalian heart. Exp Physiol, 2008: 93(2): p. 165-77

38.Schandry, R. and p. Montoya, Event-related brain potentials and the processing of cardiac activity. Biological Psychology, 1996. 42: p. 75-85.

heart beats. It is well known that HRV reflects the function and balance of the autonomic nervous system. Interestingly, research by the HeartMath Institute has found that the patterns of HRV (smooth and coherent versus jagged and incoherent) are associated with different emotional states. For example, negative emotions associated with stress, including frustration, anger and anxiety produce patterns that are erratic and irregular, referred to as incoherent. Positive emotions, such as joy and appreciation produce smooth patterns called coherent patterns. These signals from the heart to the brain affect how we process our emotions (thoughts and behaviors). **Studies show that intentional activation of positive emotions, such as appreciation, can create smooth and coherent HRV patterns that translates into resilience against stress, improved decision making, mental clarity and overall health.**

Beyond its relationship with emotional processing and cognitive function, HRV is strongly correlated with overall health and fitness. High HRV is a well-established marker of health and longevity. Reduced HRV has been linked to several clinical conditions, especially heart disease, and has been found to be a predictor of future health problems,[39] including death after a heart attack.[40] Positive[41] feelings, such as joy and appreciation, increase HRV and create a coherent state of harmony in mind and body.

Tools for measuring HRV and coherence are becoming increasingly popular for professional and personal use. There are many apps that can be downloaded onto your cellphones that can track HRV. Most of these apps only track HRV and

39. Tsuji et al, Reduced heart rate variability and mortality risk in an elderly cohort. The Framingham Heart Study. Circulation 1994. 90 (2): 878-883

40. Low heart rate variability and sudden cardiac death. journal of Electrocardiology 1988: S46-S55

41. McCraty R et al. The effects of emotions on short-term power spectrum analysis of heart rate variability. Amer J Card 1995;76(14)1089-1093

not coherence. In my office, I use a program developed by HeartMath™ to track HRV and train patients to develop coherence by tapping into positive emotions. Many of my patients have found that using the same app on their phones on a daily basis has significantly improved their coping mechanisms. By intentionally evoking positive emotions, you activate the heart-brain, the nervous system and the brain, synchronizing mind and body, a state of coherence. Studies from the HeartMath Institute suggest that higher levels of coherence are associated with resiliency against stress, greater ability to regulate emotions and behaviors and thinking clearly.

LISTEN TO YOUR GUT FEELINGS

Much like the heart, the gut has its own, independent nervous system, often referred to as the "second brain" or "gut brain." Do you ever feel "butterflies" in your stomach when you are anxious or "a knot in your stomach" when you are angry? It is the extensive nervous system in the gut that is responsible for these feelings that are associated with our stress responses. Just like the heart, the gut sends more information via the vagus nerve of the parasympathetic nervous system than it receives, and 95% of the body's serotonin is found in the gut. Serotonin is an important neurotransmitter that helps regulate mood and sleep. Many antidepressant drugs aim to increase serotonin levels. But there are many things we can do every day to naturally increase our serotonin levels. Exercise, exposure to sunshine and positive thoughts boost serotonin levels. So next time you feel the butterflies, pay attention and use your stress management tools, take a few, slow, deep breaths and evoke a positive feeling or thought.

Other useful stress management techniques include guided imagery, biofeedback, tai-chi and qigong. **As you** can see, there are many ways to manage stress. You just have to choose what resonates best with you—maybe it's going for a walk or a run, maybe it's being out in nature, maybe its yoga, meditation, mindfulness or heartfulness. Find something that you love to do and do it often and consistently for the best results.

BETTER TOGETHER

"The results you achieve will be in direct proportion to the effort you apply."
~Denis Waitley

One of the main, if not THE key underlying tenet in functional and integrative medicine is that we are all unique individuals. This bio-individuality means that there is no one-size-fits-all approach to lifestyle recommendations. Particularly when it comes to the spectrum of health to disease, individuals have different needs and different capabilities at any particular moment to adopt new lifestyle habits.

Any one thing you do to improve your heart health is fantastic and will result in reducing your risk. However, combining these different tools has an additive effect. The Ornish program, for example, consists of four key components: low-fat vegetarian diet, moderate exercise, stress management (aka yoga) and support groups. The greatest benefits in his Lifestyle Heart Trial were seen in the patients who fully participated in all four areas of lifestyle. In reality, however, this is not always possible. Choose one area that you can commit to and start there.

If we go back to the Heart Matrix, anything we do should target these five elements, or root causes of heart disease.

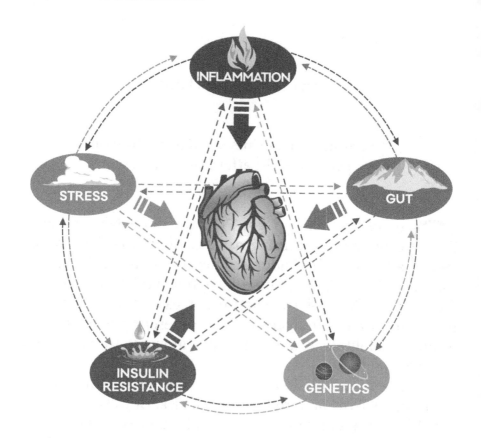

The beauty of lifestyle medicine is that any and all of these lifestyle approaches impact each and every element. For example, eating more vegetables may reduce inflammation, reduce oxidative stress, improve insulin sensitivity, improve the gut microbiome, turn on good genes, and down-regulate bad genes. Likewise, studies on yoga have shown reduced markers of inflammation, reduced markers of oxidative stress, lower levels of perceived stress, lower blood glucose and increased telomerase—an enzyme positively associated with health and longevity.[42] The same is true for exercise, meditation and good quality sleep.

---

42. Tolahunase M et al. Impact of Yoga and Meditation on Cellular Aging in Apparently Healthy Individuals: A Prospective, Open Label Single-Arm Exploratory Study. Oxidative Med Cell Longev. 2017;2017:2784153

You are in control of your health. Your heart is in your hands. Take a close look at where you are; ask yourself what are your risk factors, what are your strengths and weaknesses, and what do you need to live your best, healthiest life. Maybe it's a decision to eat more vegetables. That's great. Maybe you start here and eat a few more vegetables every day. But at the same time (especially if you're sedentary), can you make a conscious decision to move a little more, even if it's just NEAT (non-exercise activity thermogenesis) activities? Now you're getting the added benefit of two lifestyle changes without major changes to your life.

If stress is a major driver of risk for you, start with breathing and maybe meditation. To begin, sit for two minutes each day. I believe you can do that, and just two minutes each day will result in modifying the five elements. You will quickly find, however, that two minutes turns into more and you build your practice. The longer you meditate, the greater the benefits. But more important than duration is consistency. Schedule time for meditation every day. Put it on your calendar. Can you set your alarm to wake you five minutes earlier? In addition to the scheduled times, bring mindfulness with you, throughout your day. Be mindful while you eat and you will likely make better dietary choices. Be mindful while you walk—now you've combined stress management with movement and with nutrition.

To leverage your choices, consider some of the following recommendations that have been scientifically shown to reduce inflammation, reduce stress, improve insulin sensitivity, improve the microbiome, have positive epigenetic effects and thus lower your risk of heart disease.

Heart Healthy Choices:
1. **Eat REAL food and lower your intake of processed food.** Real, whole foods have not been tampered with or processed and maintain their natural goodness—vitamins, minerals, fiber and phytochemicals.

2. **Lower your sugar intake.** I'll say it again. Sugar is Enemy #1, especially from simple sugars in sweets and refined carbohydrates.

3. **Eat a rainbow of vegetables and fruit** (but more vegetables) in a variety of colors. Vegetables are full of natural anti-inflammatories, antioxidants and phytonutrients.

4. **Eat fiber.** Fiber feeds your microbiome and lowers your cholesterol.

5. **Eat wild-caught fish for their Omega-3 fatty acids.** Other good sources of Omega-3s include nuts and seeds, like chia seeds (also a good source of fiber).

6. **Consume healthy fats**, such as avocado and olive oil.

7. **Get quality sleep.** The less you sleep (even for one night) the higher the levels of CRP (marker of inflammation) and cortisol (stress hormone). Getting fewer than six hours a night has been associated with increased risk of heart disease. Healthy sleep habits can make a big difference; stick to a sleep schedule (even on weekends), practice a relaxing bedtime ritual (away from your devices and bright lights) and avoid eating for 2-3 hours before bedtime.

8. **Practice mindfulness.** Be in the moment and notice all the beauty around you. Notice how you are being and feeling in the moment. Mindfulness builds resilience to stress.

9. **Meditate.** Take a few minutes each day to meditate. Meditation builds resilience.

10. **Practice heartfulness.** Use the power of your heart to transform stress.

11. **Listen to your gut.** Those butterflies are trying to tell you something.

12. **Take up yoga.** The beauty of yoga is that you get to practice movement, breathing, mindfulness and meditation all at once.

13. **Get moving. Remember, NEAT counts.** I suggest moving once every hour.

14. **Increase your microbiome diversity.** Probiotics, fiber (which are prebiotics), fermented foods, moving regularly, getting plenty of sleep and reducing stress are all backed by research to increase your microbiome diversity.

15. **Enjoy some green tea.** Green tea is loaded with antioxidants and anti-inflammatory nutrients. Drinkers of green tea have up to a 31% lower risk of cardiovascular disease.

16. **Take it easy on the alcohol.** There's a popular belief that moderate alcohol consumption, especially red wine, is good for the heart. That is still open to debate. Heavy drinking is definitely not good for your heart or your health in general.

17. **Dark chocolate,** on the other hand, is great. Quality dark chocolate with a high cocoa count is loaded with powerful phytochemicals and antioxidants. But don't overdo it; even the best dark chocolate comes with some sugar and calories.

18. **Be positive.** Pessimists have been shown to have higher CRP levels, and optimists have been shown to have a lower incidence of heart disease. Surround yourself with positive, optimistic people. Being around negative people and being in toxic relationships will also increase levels of

inflammation.

19. **Be grateful.** Hans Selye said, "The healthiest of all human emotions is gratitude."

20. **Don't just follow your heart, lead your heart to health and happiness.**

The secret of change is to focus all your energy
not on fighting the old, but on building the new."
~Socrates

With a healthy HEART, the beat goes on . . . .

ABOUT THE AUTHOR

D r. Millie Lee, MD, FACC, MBA, is board certified in Cardiovascular Disease and Interventional Cardiology. She received her undergraduate degree in Biology from New York University and medical degree from Mount Sinai School of Medicine. She completed her internship and residency in Internal Medicine and a fellowship in Cardiology and Interventional Cardiology at Columbia Presbyterian Medical Center. She was the first female fellow in Interventional Cardiology at Columbia Presbyterian Medical Center. She is a member of the American College of Cardiology and Institute for Functional Medicine. She is a registered yoga teacher specializing in Therapeutic and Cardiac Yoga. Dr. Lee began her career as an Interventional Cardiologist, where she treated thousands of patients with heart disease. Over time, Dr. Lee became increasingly aware of the chronic nature of heart disease and the need for a more holistic approach to heart disease. She believes that heart disease can be prevented and reversed with lifestyle changes and now practices Integrative Cardiology in NYC.

MILLIE LEE, MD, FACC
www.millieleemd.com
hello@millieleemd

BOOK REVIEWS

Your Heart Is In Your Hands is the most readable, most current and most comprehensive summary of what contributes to heart disease – the #1 killer of Americans – that I have read in the thirty years I have been a doctor. As a pioneering interventional cardiologist, Dr. Millie Lee expertly blends "the science of Western medicine with the ancient wisdom of yoga." Her readable style of writing busts myths and answers essential questions about heart disease. Dr. Lee shows us how heart disease is the end result of a string of factors that we can influence and change in order for each of us to have a healthy heart that lasts a lifetime.

Liz Lyster, MD
Doctor, Best-Selling Author, Speaker
www.DrLizMD.com

In Dr. Millie Lee's great new book, cutting-edge cardiology meets holistic healing. This kind of integrative approach is the future of medicine, but with her guidance, you can have it today.

Timothy McCall, MD
Author of *Yoga as Medicine: The Yogic Prescription for Health and Healing* and *Saving My Neck: A Doctor's East/West Journey through Cancer*
Medical Editor, *Yoga Journal*
DrMcCall.com

As a patient safety activist and a daughter of a parent who died of heart issues, I have seen how intense it is to manage heart health after an event. It's much easier to prevent problems with risk management and attention to lifestyle. This book explains the five root causes called the Heart Matrix that are connected and influence heart health. *Your Heart Is In Your Hands* by Dr. Millie Lee should be mandatory reading for everyone interested in a preventive and holistic approach to achieving a healthy heart and a healthy life.

Patricia J. Rullo
Patient Safety Author/Speaker/Radio Host
speakupandstayalive.com

Dr. Millie Lee blends her Western medicine training in cardiology with her training in the ancient wisdom of Eastern medicine to create an exciting holistic approach to health and wellness. If you believe you hold the power to take an active part in preventing or reversing disease in your body, then this book is for you! Claiming that "heart disease is a lifestyle disease," the author believes that "if armed with the right information, people would make better lifestyle choices," and she sets out to do this with information on the real causes of heart disease, how they can be detected, and what to do to prevent heart disease.

Yoga pants, not drugs, may be involved.

With loads of information as well as engaging energy and passion, this book is preaching to my choir (especially coming from a career in nursing), and I feel more empowered now to make choices for myself and my family that will keep us much healthier. As an RN, much of my responsibility was patient education, and it often felt impossible to provide enough to help the patient make informed decisions.

Thank you for giving us answers in this important book, Dr. Lee.

Linda F. Patten, Leadership Trainer for Women Entrepreneurs and Changemakers – President & CEO, Dare2Lead With Linda, Website: www.dare2leadwithlinda.com, email: linda@dare2leadwithlinda.com

Additional Contact Information:
website: www.dare2leadwithlinda.com
https://www.facebook.com/dare2leadwithlinda
https://www.facebook.com/linda.patten.311
https://twitter.com/patten_linda
https://www.linkedin.com/in/lindapatten
http://www.youtube.com/c/LindaPatten
https://plus.google.com/+LindaPatten
https://www.pinterest.com/lindapatten311/

A fresh, holistic, thought-provoking, and clear exploration of heart health. Dr. Lee expertly navigates the multi-faceted nature of the heart as a physical and energetic entity as she untangles the complex interplay of body, habits, environment, genetics, mind, and spirit.

Pooja Amy Shah, MD
Integrative Medicine

Do you want to gain control of your health and well-being? Look no further than this powerful book!

Your Heart Is In Your Hands is an empowering must-read resource, and with this book by your side, your heart's health will truly be in your own capable hands. Author Dr. Millie Lee deftly guides her readers through the critical focus areas of heart health with expertise and compassion. Most importantly, Dr. Lee provides real-life answers on what to do right now to make a significant impact on your heart health and enhance your life going forward.

Wendy K. Benson, MBA, OTR/L and Elizabeth A. Myers, RN
Co-Authors, The Confident Patient
2x2 Health: Private Health Concierge
http://www.2x2health.com/

Dr. Millie Lee's leadership and holistic approach to health are exactly the medicine and hope our hearts have been waiting for. Her inspiring, innovative, patient-centered approach to heart disease is a game-changer for reversing and preventing heart disease. Dr. Millie's wonderful book is a "must-read" gem that empowers readers to transform their heart health for good!

Marlene Elizabeth, Author, Certified Money Coach® www. marleneelizabeth.com

Dr. Millie Lee masters the art of teaching scientific information in the simplest ways that anyone who reads this book will most likely understand. She states that heart disease seems nearly inevitable due to family history or the presence of other risk factors and that it can be reversed and prevented with intensive lifestyle changes. She empowers the reader to protect this very important organ in our bodies. Profound quotes are sprinkled throughout that give one pause. Dr. Lee says that you are in control of your health. Your heart is in your hands. Do yourself a favor and pick up this book to protect your heart or someone else's.

Carol Fitzgerald
Author, Health Care Advocate
www.carolfitzgerald.net
Youtube: www.youtube.com/user/thecarobi5
Facebook: www.facebook.com/carol.fitzgerald.357
Instagram: @carolfitzgerald5

This book is a timely gift, an eye- and heart-opener and a MUST read! The heart matrix and lifestyle medicine are just a couple of the many highlights. At a time when we're dealing with COVID-19 and pharma wants a one-size-fits-all approach, Dr. Millie Lee uniquely empowers the reader with ways to strengthen their relationship with their heart health and overall well-being.

Lorraine Giordano
Founder, Inspired To Health
Website: inspiredtohealth.net
Dr. Mark Hyman: Mark@ultrawellnesscenter.com